# A Young Man Goes to War - 1944

## By

## Arthur F. Adams Jr.

*To Martha*
*My Best!*
*Art Adams Jr*

ISBN: 1-4140-3688-4 (e-book)
ISBN: 1-4140-3687-6 (Paperback)
ISBN: 1-4140-3686-8 (Dust Jacket)

This book is printed on acid free paper.

1stBooks - rev. 12/22/03

## *Acknowledgement.*

My thanks go to Mr. Keith Cooley who provided the title

"A Young Man Goes to War".

I would also express my appreciation to my wife, Frances, and Mr.

Cooley for

their detailed editing work.

In addition I would also like to thank Mr. Peter Bondy for

his consultation in the German language.

# *Dedication.*

In writing this story I owe more than can ever be repaid to the key people who have formed my life. The first are my parents. They taught me how to appreciate life and make the best of whatever talents I may have. I gave them many gray hairs during my growing up period. I owe a lot to my sister whom I have always respected even though there times when we were growing up when I am sure she was not aware of this.

The person who had a profound Impact on my life over the short time I knew him was my platoon Sergeant Sim E. Cartwight. While at times I hated his guts for the way he drove me in training he taught me how to survive combat and the POW camps that followed. When he told me to do something I did it without hesitation or thought because I had implicit faith in his judgement

The person to whom I owe the most is my wife Frances, who throughout our marriage, has always supported me and given me confidence. She has also patiently listened to my stories and jokes over and over and over again throughout the years.

# *Introduction*

Throughout a lifetime each person goes through experiences that have profound impacts upon the course of their lives. Aside from my marriage I can't think of an event that changed my life more that my experience in military service. In 1944 the Second World War was well under way in both the Pacific and European theatres. In April of 1944 at age 18, I was drafted into the army. While my tour of duty was relatively short in comparison to others who served at this time it was far from dull. During my 19 months of service I was inducted into the army, trained as an infantryman, sent to Europe, fought in Germany, was wounded, captured by the Germans, liberated, injured again, recaptured and finally freed after four months in German prison camps. After a period of hospitalization I was assigned to a division that was to be trained for the invasion of Japan. Fortunately the war in the Pacific ended before this took place. I ended up as a military policeman!

It is said that we are all part of history in one way or another. I would, therefore, like to share a portion of my history with you. This is my story.

Author after Recovery.

# *Induction*

"I know what day this is and you may think this is a joke". "I assure you it isn't!" These words were spoken by an U.S. Army Major to about a thousand of us whom he had just sworn into the army at Ft. Sheridan, Illinois. It was <u>April 1</u>, 1944 (April Fools Day!) Truer words have never been spoken. The swearing-in ceremony changed me from Mr. Arthur F. Adams Jr. to Pvt. Arthur Adams serial number 36961909, Army of the United States. This would last for 19 months.

Along with the rest of my colleagues I had just been drafted. Before this time I received a nice letter from the President stating "Greeting: you are hereby directed to report for pre-induction physical examination at........" We were a strange looking bunch, all sizes and shapes. During my physical I was told that I was one pound under the minimum for my height. I asked the clerk if this would keep me out of the service. He smiled and said, "move along." For years the mere mention of the word "Greeting" would strike terror in the heart of an ex draftee.

I had already spent three or four days taking various aptitude tests and being fitted with uniforms. The uniform fitting process consisted of a supply sergeant looking at us one at a time and calling off size numbers for the supply clerks. His litany went, 7 and 1/4, 15-32, 30-32, 32 shorts medium undershirt, and so forth. He was

1

remarkably accurate. I did have a problem with under shirts; the arm openings drooped to my waist. After a few adjustments we were all fitted up and sent back to our barracks.

We each packed up our civilian clothes and sent them home. I felt as though these were my final remains being sent home to my parents. In a way they were for I would not wear civilian clothes for the duration of my enlistment. With all the strange people around me this was the first time in my life that I really felt lonely and homesick. As for the various aptitude tests given to us they were merely a formality since nearly all of us ended up in the infantry.

I should digress for a moment and tell you of my background prior to my being drafted. On Jan 4th of 1944 I was eighteen years old and by law required to register for the draft. I had graduated from high school and just finished one semester of college in Chicago. During high school I would have been considered the then equivalent of today's "electronic nerd." I don't remember the equivalent term used in those days. I was not a loner. I had several friends who were also in the "nerd" category. Since I was not athletic and couldn't compete with the "Jocks" in gym class I opted for high school ROTC (Reserve Officer Training Corp.) rather than physical education in my junior year. It was less strenuous. I laugh to think about this now since in less than three years after this I was carrying a 20 pound, 30 caliber machine gun into Germany. Also the school had a ROTC rifle shooting range in the basement and I enjoyed target practice. The school then allowed students to bring their own 22 caliber rifles to school and test them on the range. When you carried them into school you had to keep the firing mechanism in your pocket. On one occasion I brought to school an old Civil War vintage 50 caliber, cap and ball rifle I bought in the Maxwell Street ghetto to try out on the range. The range officer said no because it would be too powerful for the target racks. The machine shop instructor then helped me clean up the firing mechanism. Can you imagine doing this today?

I thought it was a rather nice touch when the members of the draft board wished me a "happy birthday" when I signed up. After registering, I boarded an elevated train for a trip down town. As I usually did I paid my 4 cents, which was half fare for children 12 and under! Even though I was 18 I was still riding public transportation for half fare. That shows you how young I looked. Later on after I was taken prisoner by the Germans, a German officer remarked that "I looked very young to be fighting a war." Since the Germans were using 16 and 17-year-old kids you can imagine what I looked like to him. Actually I was a perfect soldier candidate. I was healthy, not too bright and terrified of authority! Now the Army would mold me into well-trained, seasoned killing machine!

After three more days of processing we boarded trains for our training destination which was not divulged to us. We were assigned to dormitory type cars with bunks three high. These were essentially box cars fitted out with some windows, hooks to hang our barracks bags along with the bunks. Dining and latrine cars were also provided. We made a few stops along the way where we could get out and stretch. At a couple of stops we were treated to coffee and doughnuts by Red Cross women. After two nights and a day we arrived at our destination. As the train slowly ambled into the station we were greeted by a sign that read, "Welcome to Camp Hood Texas, Home of the IRTC".

## *Infantry Training*

I still had no idea where I was being sent or to which branch of the service I was being assigned. I was hoping that the "R" in "IRTC" stood for radio since I worked as a radio repairman before being drafted. My hopes were quickly shattered when I discovered that IRTC stood for "Infantry Replacement Training Center." I was slated for seventeen weeks of concentrated infantry training. It wasn't until I finished the 17-week training program that I realized what was meant by "Infantry Replacement". We were being trained to replace frontline casualties! This meant that we would be assigned to combat units not knowing who our buddies were or what our objectives were to be. For these reasons replacements had the highest mortality rate of any combat personnel. Fortunately for me a law was recently passed stating that 18 year-olds could not be sent oveseas as replacements. That was the good news. The bad news was that I was assigned to a division that was depleted of older men that was now made up of mostly younger men and sent off to fight.

By the time I was drafted the war had been going on for over four years. For a high school kid interested in history it was quite

4

exciting to read about the various battles and the heroic achievements of the fighting men throughout the world. Before the US entered the war in 1941 the units of the German army and navy were to be admired for their efficiency and snappy uniforms and equipment. Also, the fighting was in Europe so it wasn't our problem. When the U.S. entered the war attitudes changed. This war was probably the last of the "popular" wars. After Pearl Harbor men and women by the thousands volunteered for service. During the two and a half years since Pearl Harbor and when I was inducted I was afraid that the war would be over before I could get into it! My enthusiasm dampened somewhat when I realized what was really in store.

Upon arrival at Camp Hood we were assigned to various training companies. My organization was "Company C, 150th Infantry Training Battalion". Even though I looked young for my age I was a pretty savvy kid about getting around in rural areas and in big citys. There weren't many parts of Chicago I wouldn't go into. There were, however, some neighborhoods that I went through faster than others. Being small and thin I wasn't considered a threat to the local gangs and I quickly learned how to avoid fights. At this time I was now exposed to men from all over the country. Most of them came from the hills of Tennessee, Kentucky and Oklahoma. This was an entirely new group of people to me. Even though I lived on a farm in Missouri for a while, I was not exposed to what we then called "hill folk". Some of them couldn't read or write! I made a few dollars writing letters for them.

Our barracks were the typical WW II two story buildings put up on military posts all over the country. Each held 80 men, 40 on each floor with steel double deck bunks, foot- lockers and racks to hang your uniforms. During the war military personnel were not allowed to wear civilian clothes except when engaging in sports. The sergeant's room was one end and the latrine on the other end of the first floor. Privacy? Forget about it! The word "privacy" does not exist in any military dictionary. You sleep, fart and snore together, you eat together, you train together, you shower together, you get drunk together on the weekends, even going to the toilet is a community experience.

After we settled in we were formed into platoons and given basic organizational skills i.e. how to stand at attention, parade rest, at ease, marching and so forth. We were a rather sorry looking bunch. At this time, spring of 1944, all of the eligible men between 19 and 34 had already been drafted. Now, all that was left, were eighteen-year olds and men over thirty-five. We were read the "Articles of War" and the "Uniform Code of Military Justice". The latter covered penalties for infractions ranging from "flogging" to capital punishment. For the first two weeks we attended lectures, drilled incessantly and practiced physical exercises. Not being used to this at the end of each day I was really pooped! All this exercise gave me a ravenous appetite. Army food was good and there was always plenty of it. After evening mess several of us would go to the Post Exchange and buy pints of ice cream and devour them in minutes.

My first trip to an army dentist was a memorable one. The examining dentist decided that many of my fillings were either bad or poorly done. As a result within a 90-minute period I had 9 fillings and one extraction. Novocaine was given only for the extraction. He performed the fillings while waiting for the anesthetic to take effect. When he was finished he said, "OK soldier, back to duty". I walked out of the dispensary in a daze and sat down on the steps. A lieutenant passed by and hollered, "Soldier, don't you know how to salute an officer?" I muttered somewhat something like "what did you say?" He repeated his question and without getting an understandable response he asked, "Did you just come out of the dentist?" I responded yes and he replied, "oh forget it" and went on in.

Very early in the training program I learned to keep my mouth shut unless I was asked a direct question. For example, one morning we were lined up in the parade ground in a single file facing the field. The sergeant then said "all you men who have been to college take two steps forward". Since I had one semester of college I, along with about four or five others proudly stepped forward. The sergeant then said "those of you who have had finished high school take two steps backward". This left about fifteen men in the original rank. The sergeant then said "all you men with some college move across the field and pick up all the cigarette butts. You men with a high school education pick up all the papers.

The rest of you dumb shits go sit under a tree and watch, you might learn something."

When we began our serious training we marched to and from lectures and exercises. Often this was "on the double". Until this time I never really understood what exhaustion meant. After a few weeks I was taking things reasonably in stride. I was amazed at the physical things I could do since as I mentioned before I was not at all athletic. The most hated letters on the bulletin board daily schedule were "FFRBB". These stood for "Full Field pack, Rifles, Belts and Bayonets." The pack alone weighed about 30 lbs. Typical Army style at this time was to line up men in squads of 12 by physical size, the tallest on the right and shortest on the left. The lead man in our squad was a long, lanky 6 ft. 5in. plus man from the hills whose 30-inch stride was more like 50 inches. He was so tall that in rank he held his rifle by the muzzle while the rest of us could easily reach the stock. When ordered to "shoulder arms" he had to stoop down in order to get a grip on the weapon.

Camp Hood, now known as Fort Hood, was an enormous place perfectly suited to being an army post, as no other use could possibly be made of it. The two principal sections were known as south camp and north camp. These were separated by some 30 miles of miserable Texas countryside. This included desert scrub brush, rattlesnakes and streams that were either bone dry or 20 ft deep, and rocky ground. At one prehistoric time this area was part of an ocean bottom. It was littered with fossilized sea creatures. Flash floods were common. You were either surrounded by dust or knee deep in mud. North camp contained most of the weapons firing ranges. How did we

8

get from one camp to the other? March, of course. Going, the trip was broken into two-day segments with overnight camping. Returning was made in a one-day's march. These were all with FFRBB. Often on these daily excursions we were allowed only one canteen of water to teach us water discipline. This wasn't easy since for lunch they typically gave us two sandwiches, one containing a one-half inch slice of luncheon meat and the other containing a thick slice of peanut butter. I still haven't figured out how one can slice peanut butter! An article in Yank magazine said that proper use of a daily canteen of water included brushing your teeth, shaving, washing your face and under your arms, and washing your socks. After this, you strained the water through your under shirt and made coffee! The first couple of weeks were heavy on lectures and training films. The Venereal Disease films were quite graphic and got the point across. After these films I was afraid to even look at a girl. The "V.D." posters had ketch phrases like, "She may look clean but..." Or "Flies spread disease, keep yours buttoned!" An especially entertaining series history training film series was called "Why We Fight". These were produced and directed by Frank Capra and covered the history leading up to and into the war. By today's standards they would be considered flag waving propaganda.

It was hard for me to keep awake during lectures held outside under the hot Texas sun, since I have always had low blood pressure and tend to go to sleep especially after a heavy noon meal. When I did doze, a sharp rap on my hard plastic helmet liner by a NCO's riding crop brought me around in a hurry. On the days when steel helmets were worn you didn't dare fall asleep since once you relaxed your neck muscles and dropped your head the weight of the helmet would give you a sore neck.

Being mechanically inclined I enjoyed the sessions devoted to weapons disassembly, care and cleaning. This included the M-1 rifle, the colt 45 cal. pistol, the 30 cal. light machine gun, the BAR, and the 60 mm mortar. Mortar firing was especially interesting to me since you had to do more than just point and squeeze the trigger. They had various targets on the mortar range, one of which was an "out house". There was a reward of a case of beer to anyone that could hit and destroy it. What they didn't tell us was that the "out house" was made of fragments of tank armor welded together and live rounds merely bounced off of it. After a while the novelty of firing mortars and machine guns wore off since these weapons were heavy and we had to carry them. Also we had to clean our rifles daily and present them for inspection. One bit of dust and you were sent back to do the job over. We spent hours disassembling and reassembling various weapons often blindfolded. Later on this training paid off when I had to strip and repair my machine gun in combat.

Once we learned the mechanics of the basic weapons we went through firing exercises on the various ranges. As practice progressed, the number of times "Maggies drawers" (indicating that you missed the target) were waved over the target diminished and I was becoming a pretty good shot. These exercises were demanding but well worthwhile. Once we qualified on a particular weapon we were given decorations stating "marksman, sharpshooter, expert" and the like. One of the most stupid things I have ever done in my life was to qualify as "expert" on the light machine gun! My "Chicago background" probably helped. When I later joined a division I was made gunner on a 30-caliber light machine gun. I discovered in combat that automatic weapons drew considerable undesirable attention from the Germans.

Interspersed with our training assignments were sessions in the kitchen known as kitchen police or "K.P" duty. These came about every four or five weeks and involved a day long series of details such as washing dishes, pots and pans, floors, tables and garbage removal. Any missed training assignments had to be made up on the weekends or evenings. On one KP detail I noticed that a piece of pie had fallen to the floor. I scooped it up and dumped it into the garbage. The mess sergeant hollered at me "why did you do that soldier?" "It fell on the floor sergeant, so I threw it out." His reply was, "Soldier, if the floor isn't clean enough to eat off of, get busy"! I got the message.

After about six weeks I was amazed at the changes that occurred to me since I was drafted. I had put on weight, developed muscle and acquired considerable self-confidence. A few of the older men couldn't take the strain and were transferred to other Army organizations. The good news was that I was becoming a skilled and confident infantryman. The bad news was that I was becoming a skilled and confident infantryman! I spent two weeks in artillery school, which I liked. Even though artillery work is quite heavy, you had to do more than just point and shoot. In recognition for my prowess in artillery, however, I was sent back to the infantry!

Towards the end of our training we were given various training problems. These included night compass exercises that usually ended in confusion and chaos. We were formed into small groups and given a set of compass bearings and benchmark points that we were to use in reaching our goal. Most of us became hopelessly lost and spent the entire night wandering aimlessly about the Texas bush. We had several four-hour forced marches and one 30-mile march with FFRBB between the north and south portions of the camp. Marching troops average about 3 miles per hour with 50 minutes marching and 10 minutes of rest. It is hard to describe the degree of exhaustion one feels after a few hours march. The rest periods were a mixed blessing since after 10 minutes it was nearly impossible to get back on your feet. The sergeant would often say "off and on", which meant "off your dead ass and on your dying feet".

The infiltration course was my first real taste as to what bullets sounded like when they were whizzing over your head. We had to crawl on our stomachs under barbed wire; around obstacles, through dust clouds while machine guns sprayed live ammunition above us. It was not a comfortable feeling. River crossing training was equally hard. The two creeks named Cow and Cow house, that passed through Camp Hood, were generally mud holes used to train us for river crossing exercises. Caked with mud and struggling under

12

the stifling Texas heat not to mention the insects left a lasting impression. Often after a day's exercise we would go into the shower with our clothes stained white with salt from perspiration and black with mud. We then would scrub down our clothes and then ourselves. Some one said that in this part of Texas you could stand waist deep in mud during a snowstorm and have dust blow in your face.

The most frightening part of my training involved the use of hand grenades. We were first taught using dummies. These had the same weight and fuse timing as the real ones and were easy to throw and presented no uneasiness. Typically the real grenades were fitted with five-second fuses. The fuse was activated first by pulling a safety pin while holding down the release lever. As soon as the lever flew off, the grenade was armed and it was in your best interest to throw it as soon and far as possible! There was a tremendous fear that you might drop a grenade and freeze. When using the live grenades, we were placed in a revetment with a cadre man whose job it was to pick up and throw any grenade that you might drop, due to nervousness. We were told that it has happened, but fortunately not often. I was glad when this was over.

My introduction to the flame-thrower was also an exhilarating experience. The equipment was quite heavy and when I knelt down so the tanks could be strapped onto my back I could hardly get up. The tanks contained enough jellied gasoline for about one long 10 second burst of flame. In actual use you fired in short bursts. Squeezing the trigger brought forth a huge flame that blocked out the view of everything in front! The recoil was so strong I was afraid that I would be bowled over and incinerate the troops behind me. After two or three bursts I got the hang of it but did not relish the thought of using one in combat.

Bayonet training was taught almost as a ballet exercise. We were trained to thrust, parry and lunge in a formal matter. We lunged at straw dummies again and again. Later on a tough sergeant acted as a target daring you to stick him. He would yell and swear until you really wanted to let him have it. Any attempts, however, were quickly frustrated.

Armadillos were quite prevalent in this part of Texas. Often G.I.s would make pets of them. They aren't very affectionate but they did satisfy the need for a pet. It was not uncommon to see an armadillo walking around with "Co E." or "first platoon" painted on its shell.

My one excursion into town on a day pass was not very rewarding. The nearest town, a short bus ride away, was Kileen. Having only about 5,000 inhabitants it was overwhelmed by soldiers on the weekends and understandably not very friendly. It was nicknamed "Guadalkileen." About all you could do was drink beer and sit in the small park. The local service club was a joke, and the movie theatre was small and hot. The city of Waco was a two-hour bus ride from camp and from the comments made by other troops it was not much better. I then spent my weekends in camp reading or resting.

Staying in camp on Sundays presented some problems. You could only spend so much time in the enlisted men's club. You could shoot pool, play cards or write letters in the company day room, but you were subject to what ever work details that would come up. To avoid this, I would often go to another company's day room and tell whichever sergeant looking for men that I was visiting a friend. I also discovered that if you walked around holding a clipboard containing meaningless papers no one bothered you. It was presumed that you were on assignment.

Aside from military instruction I quickly learned many things. For example, when someone says "how about a friendly card game" you are about to lose your shirt. Also, don't lend money, it will never come back. I had most of my $50.00 monthly pay sent home in an allotment so it wouldn't be subject to the evils of gambling! Some of the men were addicted to gambling and on paydays crap and card games would erupt all over the camp. A couple of men in my platoon typically gambled away their pay in a matter of hours and spent the rest of the month begging or borrowing what they could. In the PX beer line you could only buy two bottles of 3.2 beer at a time. This meant that if you wanted more you had to get back into a long line. Since I didn't drink beer at the time I was often asked by "friends" to buy them beer. I made sure I got the money in advance!

Other things I learned were not to talk back to a corporal or sergeant; don't' call a rifle a "gun", salute officers especially second lieutenants; be nice to the supply sergeant (he is the keeper of many good things), don't upset the mess sergeant, keep your hands out of your pockets, and stay away from the orderly room. Also, most importantly, don't volunteer for anything! The first epistle to the inductee published in Yank magazine admonished, "Only the fool shall volunteer and ye shall abide in the kitchen forever!" I also learned that, when asked where I was from to reply "Illinois" and not "Chicago". If you say that you are from Illinois you were assumed to be a small town or farm boy like most of the others you encountered and were accepted. When you said that you were from Chicago you were assumed to be a "Hood" or "Tough guy. A "Hood" might have been at times but a "Tough guy' no way!

Guard duty was another of the extra details one was called on to perform. We had to memorize the 11 general orders of the guard and repeat them in order when asked. One was "walk your post in a military manner keeping everything in sight". (An unofficial variation of this order was "Walk my post in a military manner and take no crap from the company commander.") Other orders followed similar themes. A typical guard cycle was four hours on and eight hours off. We guarded warehouses, vehicles, fire alarm boxes, etc. Keeping awake during night guard sessions was quite difficult since guard duty is very boring.

Weekly inspections were held on Friday and often determined if you were eligible for a weekend pass. We were required to keep our uniforms and fatigues in a specific order, both on the clothing racks and in our footlockers. Dress uniforms were to be placed to the left and fatigues to the right. To keep a press in our dress trousers we would put them under the mattress and sleep on them. Shoes had to be polished and in order. Our footlocker contents, i.e. shorts, socks, undershirts, toilet articles etc., had to be placed in a specific order. We were allowed only the lower right hand half of the locker for personal items such as books, letters, pictures, and writing materials. Inspections were conducted either by the company commander or the platoon lieutenant. If a particular group was doing badly they were subject to "white glove" inspections. Any, repeat any, dust on the gloves worn by the inspector meant a renewed cleaning cycle. Even the openings in the metal pipes holding up the upper bunk were subject to inspections. Smokers would often pry off the metal caps in these pipes and use the pipes as ashtrays. The inspectors would often probe the pipes with long wires fitted with a piece of cloth attached, to check for ashes. If any were found the bed had to be dismantled and the pipes cleaned. Fortunately I had an upper bunk and did not smoke.

The post had several movie theatres that showed generally old films in the evening. The movie starting times were staggered from one theatre to another to allow one set of feature reels (about four or five) to be shown at all the post theatres. A typical reel ran for about 15 minutes. After a reel was shown at one theatre it was rewound and quickly driven to the next theatre. This process was repeated until all of the feature reels were shown in all of the post theatres. If a reel was late in arriving at one theatre it meant that there would be an interruption in the movie until the reel showed up. This would then affect the rest of the theatres on the post for the evening. During one scene in a really bad western I saw, the heroine knelt down in front of the hero and said, "Darling, darling, how could you forgive me for acting like this?" A soldier in the audience hollered out "My god, how could anyone forgive acting like this!" The audience along with the projectionist collapsed with laughter and the projectionist let the film run off end of the reel.

Before "graduation" there was a two-week period before we were allowed to go home on leave prior to our division assignment. Not wanting to see manpower stand around idle, we were given the choice of painting barracks or taking a two-week test for the "Expert Infantry Badge". This program consisted of a series of strenuous exercises such as log rolling, wall scaling, river crossings, marksmanship, and so forth. If you passed these tests you were entitled to wear the "Expert Infantry Badge" which was quite a symbol of achievement. Not wanting to paint barracks and impressed with my fitness, I tried out for the exercise. I grossly over estimated my physical abilities and had to drop out after four days.

When we had finished our training program we took part in a graduation ceremony. Our battalion (about 600 men) assembled on the parade ground under the hot Texas sun. Each company was photographed and then marched around the parade ground past the reviewing stand. We presented arms and accepted the commanders return salute. A short speech was given congratulating us on our successful completion of a rugged training program. This was probably one of the most significant periods of my life. I started out as a scrawny 18 year old kid and had become an 18 year old self confident and physically fit person. More important than the changes that took place in myself was the training in how to get along with others and become a part of a team. In any combat situation an individual is quite vulnerable. As a team, however, each individual becomes quite strong. I couldn't help feeling a sense of pride of accomplishment, even though now it meant that I would be going over seas to face the uncertainties of combat.

## *Home on Leave*

The train trip home following basic training was typical of train travel during wartime. Trains were crowded and often late. Hours were spent waiting in jammed terminals. At the end of training we were given travel orders instructing us where and when to report to our next unit. My orders read "Proceed to Camp Picket, Virginia and report to the personnel officer of the 78th Infantry division." I was allowed a ten-day delay en-route. If I remember correctly it took me almost two days, several trains and hours of waiting in stations just to travel to Chicago. One three-hour segment I had to sit on my duffel bag, as no seats were available. Even the "El" train ride in Chicago was crowded.

It was wonderful to see my folks since this was the first time in my life when I had been away from them. There was lots to tell and we talked for hours. Pop was in good spirits since he was happy with his job. After the long depression things were now beginning to look up. He was an architect and during the great depression the last thing the country needed was an architect. Mom was working at Sears and my sister Dorothy and her husband John were living in Rhode Island. John was a Lieutenant Commander in the Navy assigned to the Bureau of Yards and Docks.

I set about visiting friends and catching up on the latest news. Harry was home on leave from the Air Force. He had just finished training to be a machine gunner on a B-17. He was now a staff sergeant. I thought it was a bit unfair since we were both doing the same job and that he was a staff sergeant and I was only a private. Not only were we doing the same job but also I had to provide my own transportation (walking)! Spence was still selling records at Heany and Hopkins Radio and Record shop where I previously worked. The storeowner, William Faulkerson, was working full time at a defense job and conducted the radio repair business at night. I helped him out for a couple of days to clear up his backlog and earn some extra money.

Chicago was an excellent town for service people. It was impossible for a service man to pay for a drink in a neighborhood tavern because people would buy them for you. The two exceptions to this were the bars along Howard Street and Wilson Avenue, which

20

were strong military hangouts. Wilson Avenue was Army territory while Howard Street was Navy country. Transportation in busses, streetcars and elevated trains was free. Admission to neighborhood movie theatres was often free and the downtown theatres had reduced rates for service people. The downtown USO club offered free food and excellent entertainment.

To me being a soldier was still a novelty but my folks, having been through the First World War, were noticeably apprehensive. The D-Day landings had taken place just two months before and many people thought that the war in Europe would be over before Christmas. That would leave Japan alone to deal with and it would not be able to hold out against the strength of the US for long. Even though I was intrigued by the chance of seeing actual combat, I hoped that the 78th Division was headed for Europe and possible "Army of Occupation Duties" after Germany was defeated. Part of my hopes was fulfilled in that I did go to Europe but into combat and not occupation.

## *Camp Picket Virginia*

All too soon my leave was over and I set out for Camp Picket, which was located near Lynchburg Virginia. Again I faced the crowded trains and the hours of waiting in depots. Camp Picket, named after a Civil War general, was one of many temporary army posts set up during the war. The terrain was made up of rolling hills and swampland and was heavily forested. The climate in summer was hot and humid and the area was teeming with mosquitoes. Fortunately the 78th Division had just returned from maneuvers so I was spared the "joy" of spending three weeks in the rainy and muddy forest.

After initial processing I was assigned to Company "E", 310th Infantry regiment. Our barracks were the same as those at Camp Hood. Over the next few days more men reported in and we were assigned to various platoons. When my records were reviewed my prowess as a machine gunner was recognized. Strangely enough, I was assigned to a company weapons platoo! At this time an infantry rifle company was comprised of three rifle platoons, each consisting of three squads of 12 men each and a weapons platoon. The weapons platoon consisted of three-five men, 60-mm mortar squads, and two-five men, 30-caliber light machine gun squads. Based upon our platoon assignments, we were again moved to group our units together.

After the division returned from maneuvers, it was stripped of most of its complement of trained men who were then sent overseas to serve as infantry replacements. They were replaced with new men like me many of whom were only 18 or 19 years old. This was done to satisfy the critical need for infantry replacements as well as equip another division for combat. As I mentioned earlier, the casualty rates of infantry replacements was very high, Congress passed a law exempting 18 year olds from being sent overseas as replacements supposedly the extend the life expectance of the country's youths. However, there was nothing against filling up a division with 18 year-olds and sending it over seas. This is what they did with the 78th. During the First World War, the 78[th,] nicknamed the "Lightning Division", saw action in France. The shoulder patch was a red half circle with a bolt of lightning. It was now affectionately known as the "short circuit". It did achieve fame in WW II as being the first infantry division to cross the Rhine over the Remagen Bridge spanning the river in March of 1945.

Our introduction to our platoon Sergeant Sim E. Cartwright was most memorable. At 46 he was quite old for the job. He was a career army man, a Technical Sergeant, who had fought in the First World War, fought in China, fought in Panama and other locations. It seemed that he had fought with everybody! As soon as he called "attention" we knew who was boss! He was lean, ramrod straight, wore a small mustache and spoke with a strong Tennessee accent.

While we stood at attention, he walked back and forth in front of the platoon asking us our names and where we were from. After this interview he stood back and said, "this is the sorriest pile of shit I have ever seen in all of my 28 years in the army!" I imagine that he had said this many times over the span of his career, but this time I believe he really meant it! Because of the strong need for ground combat troops, many of these men had just been reassigned from the college ASTP (Army Specialized Training Program) and Air Force flight schools to the infantry. In addition, some of the men were over 35, which was old for an infantryman. Most of these men had received only six weeks of infantry training! His top machine gunner (me) looked like a kid of twelve or thirteen! With 17 weeks of training I was considered to be a pro. Sgt. Cartwright strolled back and forth in front of the platoon shaking his head. "I am going to turn you into combat soldiers even it calls for miracles!"

This is only part of the story of the composition of the 78th division at this time. As I mentioned above most of the trained older men had been transferred out after maneuvers. In my company, which was made up of about 180 men, and typical of other units in the Division, there were probably no more than a dozen regular army personnel! The rest were all draftees! This included former salesmen, farmers, truck drivers, clerks, accountants, stockbrokers, students, and lord knows what else. Our platoon Lieutenant was a furniture dealer from Iowa. Our company cook was a muleskinner from St. Joseph, Missouri.

I doubt if Sergeant Cartwright's formal education went past eighth grade and he didn't have much use for college men. As a result I didn't advertise that I had been to college but he found it out anyway. What he was smart in was how to handle men and teach them how to survive. Without his training and discipline, I do not think I would have survived combat or the prison camps that followed. When he discovered that seven or eight of us had college training, he assigned us rather colorful nicknames. Since I hope a varied audience will read these writings, I won't reveal mine.

It has been said that an army that bitches the most gets the most done. Sergeant Cartwright's philosophy was different. He made

24

it quite clear that he did not want any bitching in his platoon about how things were done. He also added, "if you want to bitch, I will give you something to really bitch about!"

The next few weeks were spent in endless marches and drills, mostly on the double. We practiced day and night tactics, attack formations in hot rainy forests filled with bugs, as well as gunnery practice. I thought I knew what exhaustion was in basic training. This was much worse. Even though Sgt. Cartwright was more that twice as old as most of us, he did every thing we did, and did not show the least bit of fatigue. He taught us not only how to be good infantrymen but most importantly, how to work and survive as a team. His lessons on survival did much to carry me through later experiences. He did say that he was impressed with my performance with the 30-caliber light machine gun on range firing. He even stopped using my nickname and called me "Adams". I took this to be a compliment.

I only went into town once while I was at Camp Picket. Lynchburg Virginia was much like Kileen Texas, a small town near an army camp that was overrun by soldiers on the weekends. I walked down the main street with a couple of my buddies and looked into store windows. There was a small park, which was crowded with GIs. In the local USO club you could borrow a 25-cent razor only if you left your cap for security. The only advantage of being in town was that here you were not subject to work details. Even though there was a dance that evening, I decided to go back to camp and try to dodge the details, again walking around with a clipboard helped.

# Trip Overseas

About-mid September the 78th division was sent to Camp Kilmer, New Jersey to prepare for shipment overseas. We were then fitted out with new equipment. By this time it was obvious we were going to Europe and not the Far East. This was a relief. I pulled guard duty one night. My post was the fire alarm box next to the P.X. It seems that some men, after a few beers took pleasure in pulling the fire alarm for enjoyment. I don't know what I would have done if there actually had been a fire.

After three or four days at camp Kilmer sitting around with nothing to do, we boarded trains for the port of New York. In any troop transport exercises it is always "hurry up and wait". We stood around waiting to get on the train, we stood around when we got off and we stood around for hours at the ferry terminal. It took an entire day to travel from the middle of New Jersey to New York harbor.

It was dark when we boarded ferryboats for the trip to our troop transport. We headed down the river toward the Queen Mary but sailed around it to the General George O. Squier, a converted oil tanker. We had hoped for the Queen Mary since it made the trip to England in 5 days. It was a 12-day trip for the Squier.

It took several hours to get all 3,000 of us settled into our compartments. Our compartment was typical of all troop transport quarters consisting of row after row of bunks, four high. Each bunk was made up of a canvas cover laced with rope and tied to a metal frame. There was 18 inches of spacing between them. A friend later commented that from his bunk he could reach out and touch 8 different men. I was assigned to a second bunk up from the bottom. It was easy to get into but the men on the bunks above me often stepped onto my bunk frame when they climbed up often waking me. On a previous voyage some creative soul had drawn a red line across the outer bulkhead of the compartment and carefully lettered the words "Torpedo depth". Very comforting.

The next evening we sailed after darkness had set in. We were ordered to stay below and not reveal any lights as we traveled down the narrows past the statue of Liberty and out into the open ocean. Some of us did sneak up on deck but with the darkness and fog all I could see were a couple of red channel marker lights. Since most of us were beat we hung up our duffel bags and climbed into our bunks. The slow rocking motion and the creaking of the ship as it passed through the ground swells and out into to sea helped put me to sleep.

Early the next morning we fell out on deck and went through abandon ship drills. I doubted that there were enough lifeboats for this large a group but hope sprang eternal. After this our sergeant briefed us on our daily schedule which included times for reveille, exercise, lectures, and various cleaning details. We were told that we would be served two meals a day and they would be scheduled at various times of the day or night. The galley operated around the clock continuously feeding troops. Unending chow lines wound around the ship. One-day

27

breakfast might be at 3:30 am. with dinner at 9:00 PM. The next day breakfast would be at 11:00 am. with dinner at midnight! If you volunteered for rust chipping and painting details for one hour a day you could have a third meal. Chipping rust was a very tedious detail and ships seem to have an endless supply of rust. I tried this once and opted for the two-meal plan. Besides, when we got out to sea the motion of the waves diminished my appetite especially when things got rough. The going joke was that we had four meals per day, two down and two up!

The latrines featured fresh water for washing and shaving. At this time I shaved only once a week. The showers used salt water. Special saltwater soap was issued because regular soap would not lather in salt water. Oddly enough, neither would the saltwater soap. The layer of salt left on your body after a shower itched for a while but I got used to it. The toilets consisted of rows of about six short standpipes each, positioned over a 10 or 12 inch diameter pipe through which ran a constant stream of water to carry things out to sea. One trick often pulled, involved the use of a fluffed up ball of toilet paper soaked with cigarette lighter fluid, which was then lighted and dropped into the upstream end of the toilet pipe. This flaming ball would progress down the pipe under the other toilet openings giving who ever was sitting a singed bottom. This would often result in fights, since not everyone appreciated the humor.

Our ship was part of a large convoy. No matter where you looked there were ships of all types in a tight formation. Escort vessels wove in and out of the convoy. During foggy weather ships trailed markers some 500 feet behind to help avoid collisions. These looked very much like the periscope of a submarine and gave some of us, me included, quite a start. We had one nighttime alert where we were ordered on deck with our life preservers. No ships, however, were attacked during our trip.

The soft rolling motion of a ship passing through calm waters was a soothing experience. The sight of seemingly endless, uneven wave patterns provided a good backdrop for reading, day-dreaming or just sleeping. Out in the-mid portion of the voyage things began to get a bit rough. While we didn't encounter any major storms the North Atlantic can be very unpredictable. On the rough days, seasickness was prevalent and helped to diminish appetites. Being turbine driven meant that the ship was free of engine vibration and noise, typical of a diesel engine and that made sleeping easy. A few compartments were fitted with hammocks. Sleeping in one takes some time and practice to get into as well get comfortable. When they are aligned with the long axis of the ship they cancel out the rolling motion of the ship since they act like a pendulum. Things are fine laying in one as long as your eyes are closed. When your eyes are open, however, you can see the side-to-side rotation of the ship. That can bring about a queasy stomach feeling.

Each morning we were awakened by a bullhorn and fell out for calisthenics on deck, rain or shine. I believe that the two most beautiful times of the day anywhere are sunset in the desert and sunrise at sea. Sunrises over the North Atlantic were no exception even when the skies were gray and overcast. Following calisthenics we were greeted by an intercom announcement, "Army sweeping crews man your brooms, clean sweep down fore and aft." I sometimes got the feeling that the navy crew considered the army troops as cargo just like tanks and jeeps.

## *England*

After 12 days our "cruise" ship reached England. We disembarked at Plymouth on October 25. A British band played American tunes as we waited to disembark. Again the routine of "hurry up and wait" prevailed. After several hours we were marched through the city to the railroad station carrying all of our gear. Civilians waved to us and one pretty young woman hollered to one of the short GIs "-eigh there shorty get out of the ole you are standing in!" We knew then we were in England.

The train ride to the resort town of Bournemouth was fairly short and we rode in passenger compartments, rather than in freight cars. When we arrived in Bournemouth it was dark. We were grouped by platoons and marched through the blacked out town to our billets. Even though the town had not suffered any air attacks just the sight of a blacked out city gave me an eerie feeling. I was beginning to realize the seriousness of what was coming and this was no longer a game.

Our billet was a private home in the Overcliff section of Bournmouth, which was a resort city on the south coast. All of the furniture had been removed and double deck bunks were placed in the rooms. Each room had "central heat", a coal burning fireplace or stove in the center of each room. The coal supplied had the consistency of sand and was hard to light. Fortunately the really cold weather had not yet settled in.

Here we were introduced to "V-mail". During the war, photographing the letters before sending solved the logistics of handling a large volume of overseas mail. The microfilm was then sent either home or to the proper overseas theater and printed for distribution. To use V-mail a letter had to be written on a special, one-page form. All letters were subject to censorship.

We stayed in Bournmouth for 26 days. Considering the times and the conditions it was a rather pleasant stay. The drill sessions were not long and the townspeople were friendly. The beach was lined with barbed wire and spotted with weapons bunkers. There was a large dance hall called the Hippodrome, which was always jammed with GIs. There was some resentment of the Americans by the British soldiers since the Americans soldiers were better paid and were dating the local girls. There was a statement in one of the British newspapers that read, "We should really be understanding of the Americans. The only things wrong with them are that they are overpaid, oversexed, overbearing, and over here!" The local pubs were friendly but some of my companions complained of the weak, warm beer nicknamed "piss quick". I believe that nearly every small town in England had a Pub named "The George and Dragon". A standing joke was to ask the barmaid if George was in. A friend noticed a sign in the men's room of a London Pub that read, "In case of an air raid, dive under the urinals, no one has hit them yet!"

Each morning we fell out before dawn and marched to the mess hall that was a converted restaurant. A Scotch brigade was also quartered in Bournmouth. Two or three times a week they marched through Bournemouth during the early morning hours to breakfast led by a group of bagpipers. It was most inspiring to us since we were already up. I am not sure that the remaining townspeople shared my appreciation however.

## *Crossing the Channel*

A few days before we were to leave for France we were again given new equipment. Some of us thought it rather strange that we were each given a dozen condoms and 5 VD prophylactic kits, but no cartridges for our weapons! One of the men asked our sergeant, "Just how are we going to fight this war Sarge?" Very early in the morning of November 21st we boarded trains for Southampton. After waiting on the docks for hours we boarded the HMS Llangibby Castle, a converted passenger ship of the Castle line. It was even more crowded than the Squier. The ship was dirty since it had not been cleaned since D-Day. The galley stank and the repetitive diet of broiled mutton and liver didn't settle well, especially since the channel crossing was rough. One man behind me in the chow line noticed a bit of blood on his slice of bread. Apparently one of the cooks cut himself in the slicing machine. I was holding my own at meals until one man threw up in his mess tray across from me. That did it! I became miserably seasick. Seasickness is an illness that is hard to describe. Nothing will stay down. First you are afraid you are going to die and then you are afraid that you are going to live! One of the troops said, when asked if he a had a weak stomach, "Hell no, it threw my dinner 20 feet!"

I lay in my bunk for a day praying for any form of relief. This came when the ship in front of ours struck a German mine while approaching Le Havre harbor. We felt our ship shudder and turn out of the channel. Barracks bags and weapons flew across the compartment as the ship heeled over. Someone said that we had been torpedoed! In no time, I was out of my bunk and up on deck completely cured! Our ship waited until the mined ship was moved out of the channel where it then settled in the shallow water. We then passed through the opening in the breakwaters and into the harbor. A large sign reading "Anchoren Verboten" (anchoring is forbidden, in German) appeared at one side of the entrance.

## *Arrival in France*

The harbor was a mess! Dozens of sunken ships and boats littered the water. A large ocean liner lay resting on its side, half submerged. The water was covered with oil and debris and the air was heavy with smoke. The harbor had been heavily bombed and had been captured only a few weeks before our arrival. The tide swing at

Le Havre is about 20 feet. As a result much of the harbor bottom was exposed and littered with refuse and sunken and damaged ships.

Since we entered the harbor at low tide, the troops had to be taken ashore in small landing boats. Scramble nets were thrown over the side and we disembarked with all of our gear. When I reached the bottom of the net, the landing craft lurched away from the ship and three of us fell into the water. We were quickly fished out but we were soaking wet and splattered with oil. As our various platoons were assembled we marched through the rubble of the completely destroyed town. The reality of war was now really sinking in.

Trucks took us to an assembly area where we pitched tents in foot deep mud. For the next two days in this area it rained constantly. It didn't make much difference to me since I was already soaked. On about November 26 we boarded "40 and 8" freight cars for the trip to Tongeren Belgium. The French countryside at this time of the year was bleak. We could have walked faster and would have been more comfortable. We made frequent stops and occasionally the locals would offer bottles of wine for sale, some of which was of questionable quality. There was a story that was passed around about a G.I. who sent a sample of local wine to a laboratory in the States for testing. The report came back stating, "We are sorry to have to tell you that your horse has severe kidney trouble".

## *Belgium*

At Tongeren we disembarked and our regiment was spread out among several small towns. Our company set up camp in a town whose name escapes me. My assistant gunner and I pitched our tent in a farmyard near an old barn. Some of the men moved into the barn along with the cattle. Our company clerk nearly got squashed when a cow rolled over on him. One of the men mentioned that the barn must be 100 years old. In the States anything 100 years is considered to be old. Here 100 years was considered to be the present. The barn was actually built in the 1600's! The town was small and consisted of only two streets lined with houses and barns. A typical set of farm and home buildings consisted of a "U" shaped arrangement with the farm house on one side of a courtyard, an equipment shed in the rear and the barn on the other side. In the middle of the courtyard was a large, steaming pile of manure! At the intersection of the two streets was located the town pump. While on KP duty I was detailed to get a bucket of water from the pump. Having lived on a farm with a well I knew that you placed the bucket under the spout and pumped the handle. While I was doing this woman approached carrying a bucket and waited patiently until I finished. She then placed her bucket under the spout and held down the pump handle. The water came gushing out without pumping; it was actually a valve. I could see by the look on her face she was thinking, "These are our liberating superheroes?"

After setting up our tent and helping to dig latrines, we set about trying to dry out our clothes and resting. Several of us posed for a combat photographer depicting a Lieutenant briefing his men on the plan of attack. The photo appeared in a service magazine sometime after the War. I chanced upon a copy of the magazine and was startled to see my image standing second from the right wearing glasses! (A copy is enclosed.) Again we performed a few close order drills; guard duty and exercises, since our platoon sergeant could not stand to see us idle. The sector we were in became known as "buzz bomb alley". This was the path of German V-1 flying bombs heading towards Antwerp. The V-1 flying bombs were small aircraft propelled by a very noisy pulsejet engine. Once you have heard the sound of a V-1 you will never forget it. They made a low droning sound that could be heard for miles. At night the red flame from the tail pipe could be seen from far off. The V-1s were guided by a simple system that wasn't too smart, and therefore they were not very accurate. They were armed with a roughly 1,000-lb. warhead and did considerable damage when they augured in.

For a couple of days the bombs came over our area every half-hour at about 1,000 ft., heading toward the harbor of Antwerp. This precise spacing had a noticeable effect upon the morale of the residents of Antwerp. When we went on guard duty at night we could count four V-1s and look for our relief. They would fly a direct path until they reached the target area and then abruptly shut down and dive to the ground with a thundering blast. One morning, at breakfast time, the "6 AM bomb" shut down abruptly over our area, but it continued to glide for a minute or two. This created pandemonium in the troops with the chow line disintegrating with men scattering everywhere. Fortunately, the bomb exploded in a field about a mile away. Occasionally fighter planes attempted to shoot them down but after one damaged bomb fell into a town the ruling were to let them alone. The RAF did have considerable success in shooting them down over the English Channel.

There wasn't much to do in the evenings except sit around and BS. There were two small taverns that served beer; wine and Calvados made from fermented apples. The beer was O.K. but the Calvados was quite powerful and caustic to my taste. I thought that "Calvadose" was the French word for "gasoline". Sergeant Cartwright once tossed a small tumbler of it into the fireplace and was greeted by a huge flame! For some unknown reason I got tired of his needling one night, and challenged the sergeant that I would match him drink for drink. This was a huge mistake! I did it, but he was in much better shape the next day than I was. This is the only time I ever knew him to show compassion. He allowed me to sleep it off the next day.

Every so often we would encounter hand drawn signs showing a face looking over a fence with the words "Kilroy was here". These would show up in the most unexpected places. No one really knew who or what "Kilroy" was but it didn't matter, it was good for a laugh. A poem that appeared in one service publication read,

"I jump with glee,

37

I jump with Joy,

I got here before Kilroy!"

Four of us were detailed to the motor pool to learn how to drive trucks. I had only driven a car a couple of times in my life but Sergeant Cartwright said that since I was a college man I shouldn't have any trouble. This is Army logic for you. I spent the morning driving a 2 and one half-ton truck around the motor pool area with an instructor, and then set off to Antwerp for supplies. I had a companion, whose job was to help load and man the 50-caliber machine gun should we encounter any German aircraft. We did encounter one low flying Junkers 88 dive-bomber but fortunately he was not interested in a truck loaded with canned milk. We made several trips over the next four days both alone and in convoy without incident and then returned to our unit. Driving in a truck convoy presents some challenges. The lead truck sets out at say 35 mph. The trucks in the center of the convoy vacillate between 25 and 45 mph., while the poor devil at the end of the convoy does 50 mph all the way just to keep up.

## *Off to the Front*

On about the 9th of December we moved out in trucks to a staging area prior to going on line. We were to replace elements of the 28th Division, which had suffered heavy casualties and was being moved back. Up to this time the army advancements through France and Belgium had been quite rapid. Now, however, we were approaching the German border, which was quite heavily defended. Our first night was spent near the Belgian town of Eupen in a dense forest. The trees were planted in rows and provided the German machine gunners with excellent targeting during the day. One could easily get lost by venturing only a few yards into the thick forest at night. Our evening meals were cold "C" rations. The "C" rations consisted of canned stews that were not bad when warm. When they were cold they were not very tasty unless you were hungry. These were augmented by "K" rations that contained biscuits, powdered coffee, cigarettes, and a Cadbury's chocolate bar. Some of the "K" rations contained supposedly high-energy "Multi-dextrose" tablets, which tasted awful. If you gave any of these to the local children they would throw them back at you, even though they were hungry.

For the next few days we were stationed in a holding area waiting to be posted to the front. We were now given ammunition for our weapons. You could hear the sound of the guns clearly especially at night. At times we could actually hear the sounds of the German tanks moving into position.

The division went on line near Roetgen, Germany on the 12th of December. We were fresh troops fitted with new equipment and no idea as to what we were getting into. The day before we went on line we discovered that some enlightened soul had given us machine gun cartridge belts fitted with tracer bullets in every fifth round. These are great for directing your fire but they point both ways! If you ever opened fire with tracers you would immediately draw the attention of the entire force facing you! As a result we spent the night replacing the tracers with ball ammunition. Even with ball ammunition you had to move quickly after firing a few bursts since machine guns were prime targets and we were facing seasoned German troops.

The regimental objective was to capture a series of dams on the Roer River to prevent the Germans from blowing them up, thereby flooding out the British in Holland. Our first goal was to capture the town of Simereth, not far from Rotgen near the Belgian/German border. Simereth was essentially a one street town of probably less than 200 residents. It was heavily fortified when the 28th Division captured it. As a result it was severely damaged. This was the beginning of the German line of defense named "The Siegfreid Line". This line of fortifications extending from France through Holland was comprised of gun emplacements, huge "dragon's teeth" concrete tank barriers, barbed wire and other defense elements.

We first passed through the town of Lammersdorf and encountered only sporadic firing. We were warned not to use any German foxholes since they might be booby-trapped. A pillbox on the road to Rollesbroich was causing trouble for our neighboring battalion but we were not bothered by it. It was eventually put out of action. As we moved into position, elements from the 28th Division moved to the rear and we took their positions. The opposition was not too fierce on the first day and we spent most of the time mopping up and looking for snipers.

It is hard to describe the feeling you have when you enter into a combat area for the first time. There is an aura of excitement and "damn the torpedoes" attitude combined with extreme nervousness. While we were advancing on foot to Simereth, we passed about dozen-wounded men on their way back to an aid station. My mood then changed to one of apprehension and fear!

It was eerie moving through the overcast town with no one in sight. The civilians had all scattered to the forests to wait out the action. Buildings were burned and damaged by shellfire, trees stripped bare, a dead horse lay in the street, along with miscellaneous wreckage. In our imagination every house window contained a sniper. Unfortunately this was partially true. When a sniper killed our Company clerk everything changed rapidly. We were then detailed into small groups tasked with eliminating the sniper or snipers. Since I was a machine gunner my squad was tasked with providing cover for the search teams. It wasn't long before the sniper was discovered and killed. The remainder of the day was spent in digging foxholes on the outer edge of the town. Since winter was beginning to set in, the ground was beginning to get hard but it is amazing how fast one can work when someone is taking pot shots at you. . It was curious how oblivious farm animals were to the war that was going on around them. Chickens roamed around looking for seeds; a cow stood in a pasture chewing her cud. Occasionally they were "spooked" by gunfire. Signs reading "Achtung Minen" marked many fields. The Germans often put these "Danger Mines" signs in areas that were not even mined but you could never be sure. A horse wandered about one supposedly mined field without setting anything off. After I was liberated and on my way home, I saw an "Achtung Minen" sign in the men's room of a Paris bar! While selecting a spot for my foxhole, I spotted a mine in the location where I wanted to dig. I chose another spot!

During the night, a couple of squads of German Infantry crept into town. Fortunately they were spotted before they got very far and we routed them in a short fight with only one casualty. After digging in along a hedgerow on the far side of the town we given today's password and took turns pulling guard duty. I don't know which was the more frightening situation, active combat or the quiet between actions. Combat is not always like it is shown in the movies. Much of the time is spent in boredom with only the occasional pop of rifle bullet passing overhead to bring you out of complacency. Sporadic artillery and mortar barrages kept us on our toes. When real action took place the noise was deafening. The winter cold was just beginning to set in and we had not yet been issued winter clothing. Our combat jackets were barely adequate to keep out the cold especially at night when on guard. One of the biggest causes of casualties among American troops during the winter campaign was trench foot. This was caused by a combination of cold and wetness. The effect was to cause severe pain in the feet which often led to amputation of toes or the feet themselves. Frostbite was also a problem.

Our advance was cut short by a German counter attack that was possibly linked to the Bulge offensive which took place to the north of us a few days later. On the evening of December 14 our company was tasked to capture and occupy the town of Kesternich about 1 km from Simereth. This town held a commanding view of the valley beyond. During the day both of us machine gunners fired over 1,000 rounds of ammunition into the town in an attempt to soften things up. A concrete bunker was located on the road leading into Kesternich. This was making things very difficult, to say the least. We called for tank support and after several hours three Sherman tanks moved up only to be knocked out by an 88-mm gun in the bunker. We were then left to our own resources. Our company was distributed along both sides of the main road leading through Simereth. The bunker held a commanding view right down the road. If we tried to cross the road we drew immediate fire from the bunker. Pumping machine gun rounds into the bunker had little or no effect except to make the Germans mad. To get around this we had to backtrack through the houses and barns, about 200 yards, to a bend in the road where we could then safely cross. Even at this our company suffered severe casualties.

## *Kesternich*

In the very early morning, about 1 AM of the 15th of December, one rifle platoon and part of the company weapons platoon set out to bypass Kesternich and its bunker and set up on the opposite end of the town, a distance of about one-half mile. The remainder of the company was to advance through the town and join up with us the next day. We started out in small groups traveling along a series of hedgerows paralleling the town. Fortunately the night was overcast and quite dark. We hoped that our silhouettes against the light snow background would not give us away. All we could see of the houses along the main road of the town were their outlines. I couldn't help feeling that each house contained a squad of German soldiers ready to open fire on us. We moved as quietly as possible cutting wire fences where needed. I cringed every time a twig snapped. The trip which, probably took maybe a half an hour, seemed like an eternity. Just as our patrol reached the far end of the town the Germans opened up with mortar fire. I was hit by a mortar fragment in the knee and my foot was injured by falling masonry from a building hit by a mortar round. My injuries were not serious but they were painful. We quickly dispersed and took up positions on the outer edge of the town and dug in. No further action took place until dawn.

Even with the earlier mortar fire some German soldiers seemed unaware of our advance. Just after dawn two German soldiers walked up the road into town apparently returning from leave and into our hands. They were wearing garrison caps and their rifles and helmets were slung over their shoulders. Startled, they dropped their weapons and became prisoners. After setting up our machine gun positions and had begun digging in, we observed a German mess truck serving breakfast to the troops about 500 yards away. Along with the second machine gun crew, I opened up on them with good results. They panicked and fled in all directions and were obviously upset at having their breakfast interrupted and provided an immediate mortar and artillery response, which resulted in no casualties.

Unfortunately the remainder of our company was unable to rout the Germans from the other end of the town and was pinned down for most of the day. This left our group with hostility on two sides, which was not a desirable situation. About mid afternoon two huge German tanks advanced up the road into the outer edge of the town. They began firing at company positions on the West End of town. One tank took up position on the road not more than 75 ft from my hole but there wasn't much I could do about it since a light machine gun is nothing more than a minor irritant to a tank! I wished that I had dug my hole ten feet deeper. After about fifteen minutes the tanks withdrew spraying the ground around them with machine gun fire. The rest of the afternoon was relatively quiet except for gunfire directed at the rearward portion of our company. They were still pinned down at the West Side of town and took heavy casualties. We now had strong German forces on both sides of us.

The rest of the day was spent in sporadic fire from both sides keeping us pinned down in our foxholes. In the evening what was left of the forward group moved into a couple of damaged houses for the night. We surveyed our ammunition supply and distributed what little was left. Six or seven men were wounded. Lookouts were posted and we were well aware of the fact that we were now very alone since the rest of the company had failed to take the town behind us. My foot was beginning to ache and I fell asleep in the basement of the house. Just at dawn German infantry advanced on the outer houses and began firing. An artillery round exploded in the entranceway of the house I was in, leaving a large hole in the side of the house where the door had been. Since several of us were wounded and we were nearly out of ammunition we surrendered.

German soldiers began rousting out the other members of our company from the adjacent houses. They set fire to a couple of haystacks since these could be used as hiding places. Sgt. Cartright was captured alone with the rest of us. Seeing him standing with his hands on top of his head I thought what a poor ending for his remarkable career. I even felt that I had let him down. The discipline and teamwork he impressed upon me now helped me survive prison life. Kesternich was then retaken by the Germans who held it through the winter until early February. During this time in this battle for Kesternich, the second battalion, of which company E was a part, lost 542 men killed, wounded or captured. This was out of a total personnel level of 650! The three rifle companies lost all of their officers.

Stepping through the gaping hole that had once been a door of the house on that cold overcast morning, it seemed as though I was stepping into another world. In fact I was!

# ILLUSTRATIONS

*Arthur F. Adams Jr.*

48

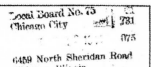

APP. not req.

SELECTIVE SERVICE SYSTEM

Order to Report
Preinduction Physical Examination

Local Board No. 75
Chicago City              781
                          875

6459 North Sheridan Road
Chicago, Illinois
(LOCAL BOARD DATE STAMP WITH CODE)

February 19, 1944
(Date of mailing)

*The President of the United States,*

To ___Arthur___ ___Frederick___ ___Adams, Jr___ ___13056___
   (First name)    (Middle name)    (Last name)    (Order No.)

GREETING:

You are hereby directed to report for preinduction physical examination at

6459 Sheridan Road    Chicago, Illinois
(Place of reporting)

at ___9:00___ Am., on the ___26___ of ___February___, 1944
(Hour of reporting)    (Day)    (Month)

*Camilla McDonough*
(Member or clerk of Local Board)

### IMPORTANT NOTICE TO REGISTRANT

Registrant who believes he has a disqualifying defect.—If you believe that you have some defect which will disqualify you for service you may, on or before the ___25___ day of ___February___, 194_4_, appear in person at the office of the Local Board, or, if you are unable by reason of such defect to personally appear, you may submit an affidavit from a reputable physician or an official statement by an authorized representative of a Federal or State agency to the effect that such physician has personal professional knowledge or such authorized representative has official knowledge of your defect, the character thereof, and that you are unable to personally appear due to the character of the defect. The Local Board may send you to the Local Board examining physician, and, if it does so, it shall be your duty to appear at the time and place designated by the Local Board and to submit to such examination as the examining physician shall direct. If the Local Board determines that your defect does disqualify you for service you will receive a Notice of Classification (Form 57) advising you that you have been placed in Class IV-F. Unless prior to the date fixed for your preinduction physical examination, you receive such a Notice of Classification (Form 57) advising you that you have been placed in Class IV-F, you must report for your preinduction physical examination as directed.

Every registrant.—When you report for preinduction physical examination you will be forwarded to an induction station where you will be given a complete physical examination to determine whether you are physically fit for service. If you sign a Request for Immediate Induction (Form 219), and you are found qualified for service, you will be inducted immediately following the completion of your preinduction physical examination. Otherwise, upon completion of your preinduction physical examination, you will be returned to this Local Board. You will be furnished transportation and meals and lodgings when necessary. Following your preinduction physical examination you will receive a certificate issued by the commanding officer of the induction station showing your physical fitness for service or lack thereof.

If you fail to report for preinduction physical examination as directed, you will be delinquent and will be immediately ordered to report for induction into the armed forces. You will also be subject to fine and imprisonment under the provisions of section 11 of the Selective Training and Service Act of 1940, as amended.

If you are so far from your own Local Board that reporting in compliance with this order will be a hardship and you desire to report to the Local Board in the area in which you are now located, take this order and go immediately to that Local Board and make written request for transfer for preinduction physical examination.

DSS Form 215

16—27079-1    U. S. GOVERNMENT PRINTING OFFICE

# Draft Notice.

**DAILY TRAINING SCHEDULE**
**91st Inf Repl Tng Regt**

150th Tng Bn   From: 5 June 1944

| 9th Week | Co A | Co B | Co C | Co D | SUBJECT | REFERENCES | PLACE | UNIFORM |
|---|---|---|---|---|---|---|---|---|
| **Mon, 5 June** | 0730-0900 | 0730-0900 | 0730-0900 | 0730-0900 | Orientation | "Battle of Russia" | 162nd St Th | C |
| | 0900-0930 | 0900-0930 | 0900-0930 | 0900-0930 | (OT) Subject to be announced later | | A,C M-2; B,D M-3 | As Prescribed |
| | 0930-1030 | 0930-1030 | 1030-1130 | | Phys Tng | IRTC Rgt Slip; TC 87 | Obst C | C w/CPRB |
| | 1030-1130 | 1030-1130 | 0930-1030 | | Dismt'd Drill | SS #61 Sec II Per 14 | M-2 | C w/RBB |
| | 1300-1400 | 1300-1400 | 1300-1400 | | (OT) Subject to be announced later | | Co Area | As Prescribed |
| | 1400-1500 | 1400-1500 | 1400-1500 | | Inspection | SS #73 Sec II Per 8 | Co Area | As Prescribed |
| | | 1500-1700 | 1500-1700 | | Free Time (See Recap) | | Co Area | |
| | 0930-1700 | | | 0930-1700 | LMG Mkms Tng | SS #27 Sec IV Pers 1, 2 | K-2 | C w/RB |
| | | | | | 60mm Mkms Tng | SS #30 Sec IV Per 1 | M-3 | C w/RB |
| **Tues, 6 June** | | | 0730-0830 | | Phys Tng | IRTC Rtg Slip; TC 87 | Obst C | C w/CPRB |
| | | | 0830-0930 | | Phys Tng (See Notes) | (Same) | K-2 | C |
| | 0930-1030 }<br>1300-1400 } | | | | (OT) Subject to be announced later | | B & C in K-2; A Co 0930 in M-2 1300 Co Area | As Prescribed |
| | 1030-1130<br>1400-1500 | | | | Dismt'd Drill | SS #61 Sec II Per 14 | M-2 | C w/RBB |
| | | | | | Inspection | SS #73 Sec II Per 8 | Co Area | As Prescribed |
| | 0730-0930 | | | | Bayt (Review) 1 hr<br>MTP 3-3, Per 4; 1 Hr<br>Group Assault Tactics | FM 23-25, Sec III;<br>MTP 3-3, Sec I, Per 4 | K-2 | C w/RBB |
| | | | | 0730-1700 | Con of Phtls | SS #72 Sec V Pers 6 & 7 | 1-3 | C w/FFRBB |
| | | 0930-1700 | 0930-1700 | LUNCH IN THE FIELD | LMG Mkms Tng | SS #27 Sec IV Pers 1, 2 | K-2 | C w/RB |
| | 1500-1700 | | | | 60mm Mkms Tng<br>Free Time (See Recap) | SS #30 Sec IV Per 1 | M-3 | C w/RB |

Typical Daily Training Schedule.

Gen. Squier Class Troopship.

The Team
(Author Standing Second from Right)

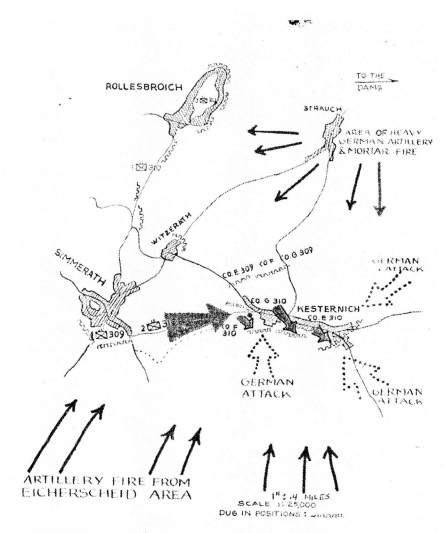

## BATTLE of KESTERNICH ~ DEC. 15

A Town Like Kesternich.

Cologne in 1945.

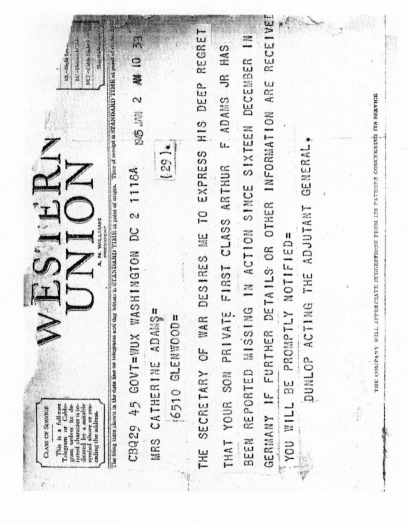

## WESTERN UNION

A. N. WILLIAMS
PRESIDENT

CBQ29 45 GOVT=WUX WASHINGTON DC 2 1116A 1945 JAN 2 AM 10 53

MRS CATHERINE ADAMS=
'6510 GLENWOOD=

THE SECRETARY OF WAR DESIRES ME TO EXPRESS HIS DEEP REGRET

THAT YOUR SON PRIVATE FIRST CLASS ARTHUR F ADAMS JR HAS

BEEN REPORTED MISSING IN ACTION SINCE SIXTEEN DECEMBER IN

GERMANY IF FURTHER DETAILS OR OTHER INFORMATION ARE RECEIVE

YOU WILL BE PROMPTLY NOTIFIED=

DUNLOP ACTING THE ADJUTANT GENERAL.

M.I.A. Telegram

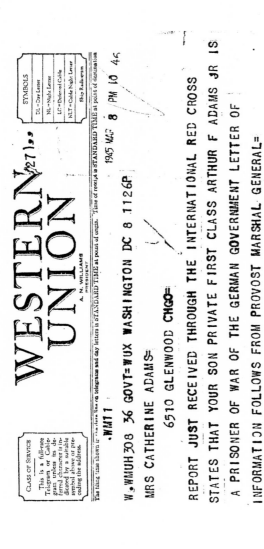

## WESTERN UNION

CLASS OF SERVICE

This is a full-rate Telegram or Cable-gram unless its de-ferred character is in-dicated by a suitable symbol above or pre-ceding the address.

A. N. WILLIAMS
PRESIDENT

SYMBOLS

DL = Day Letter
NL = Night Letter
LC = Deferred Cable
NLT = Cable Night Letter
Ship Radiogram

The filing time shown in the date line on telegrams and day letters is STANDARD TIME at point of origin. Time of receipt is STANDARD TIME at point of destination

.WM11

W.WMUH 308 36 GOVT=WUX WASHINGTON DC 8 1126P

1945 MAY 8 PM 10 46

MRS CATHERINE ADAMS=

6510 GLENWOOD CHGO=

REPORT JUST RECEIVED THROUGH THE INTERNATIONAL RED CROSS

STATES THAT YOUR SON PRIVATE FIRST CLASS ARTHUR F ADAMS JR IS

A PRISONER OF WAR OF THE GERMAN GOVERNMENT LETTER OF

INFORMATION FOLLOWS FROM PROVOST MARSHAL GENERAL=

J A ULIO THE ADJUTANT GENERAL.

THE COMPANY WILL APPRECIATE SUGGESTIONS FROM ITS PATRONS CONCERNING ITS SERVICE

## P.O.W. Notification.

57

Newspaper Casualty List.

# PRISONERS OF WAR BULLETIN

Published by the American National Red Cross for the Relatives of American Prisoners of War and Civilian Internees

VOL. 3, NO. 5          WASHINGTON, D. C.          MAY 1945

## Reports on German Camps

With events inside Germany occurring at such speed that even the daily newspapers are barely able to keep the record up to date, readers will appreciate that a monthly publication which tries to keep abreast of changes in the prisoner of war picture is now laboring under a great handicap. PRISONERS OF WAR BULLETIN, moreover, must be quite sure of the facts it reports. The time element in a publication of this character is a less important factor than strict accuracy or believe.

Our main source of information on camp conditions, movements of prisoners, and delivery of relief supplies is the International Committee of the Red Cross, which is not a news gathering organization. Its major functions now are to get the supplies into the hands of prisoners of war, and to urge belligerents in every way possible to comply with the provisions of the Geneva Convention. Its entire staff is working literally day and night to perform these tasks, and, when all the difficulties are taken into consideration, it is rendering a remarkable degree of success.

Recent instances of flagrant violations of the Convention by Germany have been reported to the prisoners. There are examples and censorship, but, at the same time, it may be noted that the German authorities in some instances have done more than was required of them under the Convention in facilitating the delivery of relief supplies to prisoners in Germany. There are now several hundred Red Cross trucks, traveling under German escort and driven, in many cases, by Allied prisoners of war, carrying out their relief mission right in the heart of the enemy's territory. The architects of the Geneva Convention could never have foreseen such a situation as has developed inside Germany, but the guardians of the Convention are doing everything humanly possible to meet it.—Editor.

### Stalag VII A

The total camp strength at Stalag VII A, Moosburg, when visited by a Delegate of the International Committee of the Red Cross on January 27, was 77,249, of whom 14,943 were in the base camp. The remainder were on work detachments. The total of 77,249 included 42 American officers, 238 noncoms, 5,708 enlisted men, and 3 medical officers. Since January 27, however, many Americans from camps in the east, and particularly from Stalag Luft III, have reached Stalag VII A, and cables received in March stated the camp strength exceeded 100,000. During March large shipments of food and other supplies reached Stalag VII A from International Red Cross warehouses in Switzerland, both by rail and by truck convoys, to meet the rapidly growing need.

On January 27 the Americans at Stalag VII A had a five weeks' reserve of standard food packages, but new arrivals at the camp quickly disposed of this reserve supply. The principal grievances of the men at the end of January were reported to be overcrowding, which has since grown worse, lack of fuel for cooking, and inadequate bathing facilities. The camp theater was being transformed to accommodate new arrivals.

Detachments of from 1,000 to 2,000 men were sent daily (Sundays excepted) by train from Stalag VII A to work in Munich. They returned by train the same day, travel time and work consuming about 12 hours.

### Stalags V A and V B

On January 9 an International Red Cross Delegate visited Stalag V B, at Villingen, in southwest Germany not far from the Swiss border. The camp then held 479 Americans in transit from the western front. The men had reached Stalag V B, the Delegate's report stated, in an exhausted condition after a four-day hike. From Stalag V B American prisoners were being transferred to Stalag V A, at Ludwigsburg, in the vicinity of Stuttgart.

A later report from the Interna-

*A truck convoy entering Germany, from Switzerland, with Red Cross supplies for prisoners of war. The trucks are painted white to increase visibility. They also carry the Red Cross emblem and the flag of Switzerland to ensure protection.*

## Red Cross Prisoner of War Bulletin.

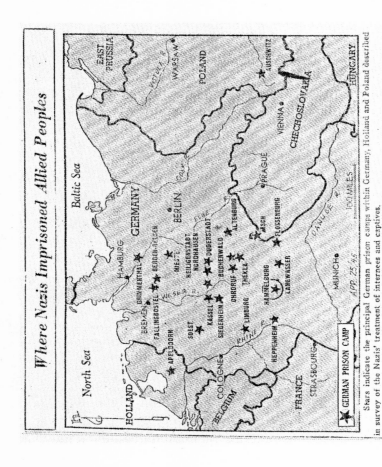

*Where Nazis Imprisoned Allied Peoples*

Stars indicate the principal German prison camps within Germany, Holland and Poland described in survey of the Nazis' treatment of internees and captives.

Location of Major German POW Camps.

Hammelburg Liberated

# Author as a Fearless Military Policeman!

# *Prisoners*

When I left for overseas I had thoughts about being wounded, disabled and even killed but I never imagined that I would become a prisoner. During my furlough I told my parents that I would probably be part of the army of occupation since we all thought the war would be over by Christmas. All that changed for me on that morning of December 16th.

The German soldier who took my pistol waved it around to motion us to move. I was afraid that it would go off since I kept it loaded and cocked! Once they had assembled a group of us, they marched us off into Germany. We traveled to a barn about a mile away and were held there for several hours. Altogether 38 men were taken prisoner from our portion of the company, nine of whom were wounded. After a while it became very relaxing holding your hands on top of your head. I noticed that some of the belt buckles worn by the German soldiers had the inscription "Gott Mit Uns" (God is with us). I was beginning to wonder whose side he was really on.

We were then loaded into trucks and driven to the town of Duren. Some of us were ushered into an empty room and told to sit on the floor. We stayed there most of the day waiting to see what was next. A German soldier posted in the room to watch over us had an old wind-up phonograph and periodically played records. One of the records was a British parody record entitled "We Will Hang out the

Washing on the Siegfreid Line". The "Siegfreid line" was the name given by the Germans for the elaborate fortifications developed along the German border. This broke us up with laughter. The soldier was pleased that it entertained us. He must have captured the record during the fall of France and had no idea as to what it meant. Sleep was hard to come by since the flood was hard and by foot and knee ached. Early the next morning we were told to move out where we joined other prisoners. Four of the wounded prisoners were too weak to walk. A German officer told us that transport would be arranged for those who were unable to walk. I was tempted to stay because my foot was beginning to ache badly but something told me that I shouldn't. We heard later that the men who stayed behind were shot. I could never verify this but I did not see any of them again.

For about five days we walked in a northeasterly direction before being turned south towards Cologne. During this march we joined other prisoners from the 106$^{th}$, 28$^{th}$, 99$^{th}$, and 82$^{nd}$ and 101$^{st}$ Airborne Divisions who were swept up in the battle of the Bulge.

By the time we reached a transit camp near Bonn there were over 3,000 in our group. During this march we were fed twice on some bread and potatoes. While we were on the march, a guard handed one of the men an apple. He took a small bite out of it and passed it back. Each man then took a tiny bite and passed it back until it was gone. We slept, or tried to sleep, out in open fields on two freezing nights. On one night it snowed lightly. We huddled together and jumped up and down to keep warm. As I mentioned before, we had not yet been issued winter uniforms. All we had were our combat jackets. Several men from the other divisions who had been wounded and could not keep up died along the way. We were not given many rest periods since the guards became uneasy when the group was not moving. One British soldier was shot in the head by a German Lieutenant simply because he could not keep up. This episode encouraged us to keep moving. Twice we were briefly strafed by low flying British and American fighter planes before they realized that we were prisoners. After the second attack two P-51 Mustangs circled our group several times before heading for home base.

In Chicago where I grew up, there was a large number of people of German ancestry. They had a reputation of being hard working, hard playing, likeable, and jovial people. This image changed over the next few days. It appeared that these same jovial, fun loving people had suddenly become quite brutal!

At first the experience of being captured was a relief from the noise and brutality of combat. Also there were many of us together which was reassuring. When I was captured, I was only 18 and very young and idealistic. At one point several German officers reviewed our column shortly after capture. A high ranking German officer who looked as though he was 9 feet tall in his black leather overcoat remarked to me that I was very young to be fighting a war and asked me how old I was. I was nearly too frightened to answer. Since they were using 16 and 17 year-old boys this showed how young I looked.

He probably thought that the Americans must now really are scraping the bottom of the barrel.

We were kept marching through much of the daytime with periodic short time outs for rest. When we were reassembled we were again grouped in lots of 50. Guards on both sides of the columns often counted each group. At the end of each count they would invariably have different numbers and we had to be counted all over. Once reassembled we continued our march. The guards constantly pressured us with "Los, Los." And "Mach Schnell!" We were hurried through towns since it was easier to escape in the confusion of streets and houses. Civilians watched us curiously with only slight open hostility. The few airmen in our group were advised to remove any insignia and march in the middle of the groups.

## *Work Details in Transit*

After the third or fourth day our group of about 100 men stopped in a small town to await regrouping with other prisoners. We were housed in an empty warehouse. Even though there was no heat in the building it was a relief from the overcast winter cold. The floor was covered with straw and a large barrel was provided for use as a latrine. In the afternoon several of us were transferred to a first aid station that was treating German wounded. Here we carried stretchers, cleaned up the rooms, emptied bedpans, and brought in firewood. Some of the men were severely wounded. It was there that a German soldier gave us Red Cross post cards to fill in. These were later sent home.

In the afternoon about ten of us were transferred to a bakery that was baking bread for the army. The bread was molded into one-kilo loaves and placed onto long boards. The day's date was then stamped on top of each loaf. The dough looked like wet Portland cement. When about a dozen loaves were placed on the board, we carried it out to the oven for baking. The baking was a continuous process, when we placed one board into the oven another was removed. After baking, the loaves were taken to a barn where they were stacked for aging. It was tempting to take a bite out of one but we were told that the bread must age for about 30 days before it can be eaten or it will make you sick. The loaves looked much the same after they came out of the oven as they did when they went in. Each loaf was about 5 by 5 by 12 inches and weighed one kilo. There was a crust on top but that was the only obvious difference. The Kriegsgefanen Lager Brot (war prisoner camp bread) was made with roughly one third rye flour, one third wheat flour, one third potato flour, five percent sawdust used as a binder, and boric acid as a preserver. It was a heavy bread that tended to fill you up in a hurry. How nourishing it was I couldn't say.

We crossed the river Rhine at Cologne on a pontoon bridge, since the permanent bridges had all been destroyed, and were marched through the burned-out city. The blackened cathedral stood out above the ruined buildings. H

There, the civilians became openly hostile, and we were told to move quickly. It was jokingly said that the 106th Division was the first American division to cross the Rhine River (as prisoners).

The transit camp at Bonn shocked me into my first realization as to what was ahead of us in prison. Next to our camp was a compound for Russian prisoners. These were Russians for whom the Germans either had no work or they were prisoners they couldn't handle. The men were actually being left to starve. One emaciated Russian soldier held out a violin through the fence in an attempt to trade it for food from the Americans. We had nothing to give him. The morning after our arrival I watched a horse drawn cart move through the Russian compound and collect the bodies of men who had died during the night. What little food that was given them was brought in under guard in large vats and left for the men to fight over.

From Bonn we were transported by train with some 40 to 50 men crowded into each boxcar to our next camp. A large bucket placed at the end of each boxcar to serve as a latrine. To keep warm we huddled together and sang to keep up our spirits. The first night we traveled for only a couple of hours. While parked in the railroad station at Koblenz the British decided to bomb the rail yards. This was Christmas Eve. We even though our train was not hit; the explosions shook the cars violently. Most of us sang Christmas carols to help keep up our spirits. At the end of every third or fourth boxcar was a small shack occupied by a guard or brakeman. I kind of felt sorry for him for it must have been colder out there than it was inside the cars. After spending a day and a night aboard freight cars we were allowed to disembark at a station near Limburg under heavy guard. . We were originally slated to be sent to Stalag 12A near the town of Limburg but on Christmas Eve the British accidentally bombed the camp during the same raid upon Koblenz. . This was Christmas day. At this time there were about 1,500 of us. After spending the day jumping up and down to keep warm on the cold snowy station platform we again boarded the train for the trip to Hammelburg. We traveled mostly at night since moving trains were easy targets for American and British fighter aircraft during the day. The trains were not marked indicating that they contained prisoners.

## *Stalag XIIIC Hammelburg*

We arrived at the town of Hammelburg after midnight. We disembarked and were marched through the streets to a camp just outside of town. It was an eerie experience since it was cold and no residents were awake except for a lone old man who watched us with disgust from a street corner under a dim streetlight. We matched through the town and up a road leading to the camp. We stopped for a while so that the guards could get coffee from a canteen.

The camp, Stalag XIIIC, was located just outside of town and at one time was an army post probably built at the time of the Emperor Bismark. The word "Stalag" is short for "Stamlager" which means "Enlisted Man's Camp." We later discovered that there were several thousand other prisoners housed there including Russians,

French, British, Poles, Yugoslavs, and even Italians who, at one time, were allied with the Germans. Upon arrival at the camp we were strip-searched in a very cold room. I was allowed to keep a small religious badge, which they stamped "Gepruft", approved in German. We then filled out papers for the Red Cross and were given identity tags. The tag was made of metal and was serrated down the middle. It read "Stamlager XIIIC KG 19276. I now had a new serial number! I later found out why it was serrated. If you should die while a prisoner, they would break the tag in half, nail one half onto your coffin and send the other half to the Red Cross. This was very comforting to know. I thought it curious that one of the papers we had to sign stated that we would not have any relations with German women while a prisoner. They needn't have bothered since when you are starving, keeping company with a woman is the last thing that is on your mind. Here we filled out cards to be sent to our relatives telling them where we were.

My tour of duty as a Kreigsgefangenen (German for prisoner of war) was relatively short. The events I experienced, however, were probably typical of other POW's captured late in the war. My imprisonment was divided between camps designated Oflag XIIIB and Stalag XIIIC where I was put to work on various jobs, and assignments to "Arbiets Kommando" (work details) outside the camp. These details were tasked to clear bomb damage and repair railroad tracks. A map, attached, shows the location of major POW camps including Stalag XIIIC at Hammelburg.

Living conditions in the German prison camps varied depending upon how long the camp had been established. Conditions in camps which had been in existence for several years were considerably better, (certainly not ideal) than those in camps, like Stalag XIII C, which had been open for only a short time to Americans. Living conditions at Stalag XIIIC were poor. The food was marginal, the buildings were poorly heated and lice were everywhere. Established camps had some access to reading material and occasional Red Cross food parcels. Neither of these was available to any extent at Hammelburg. These, however, didn't do much to overcome the boredom of long-term imprisonment and not having the freedom to move about. My tour as a POW, though short, was seldom boring.

At this point I feel that I should digress and talk about the impact of the war upon the home front, and the effect of hearing a loved one has been reported, "Missing in Action". As I mentioned above, it never occurred to me that I would be reported, missing.

I didn't prepare my parents for that event. Actually, during the war the vast majority of troops reported "missing" either turned up in other organizations or became prisoners of war. The notice of my being missing was sent by telegram. It arrived on my birthday! It couldn't have come at a worse time.

Throughout the war newspapers ran daily accounts of combat casualties, killed, wounded and missing. As the war neared the end, good news was also published on the persons captured or freed from

POW camps. My name appeared in both of these categories. The telegram notifying my parents that I was prisoner arrived in April about a week after the postcard I sent from Germany in January.

While I was in high school I developed an interest in listening to short wave radio broadcasts from Europe and the Far East. The German overseas radio presented daily news reports in English laced with propaganda. The propaganda style was crude by today's standards. The hourly news and propaganda program would start out with the slogan, "The world is divided into two camps, in the one camp is Jewish bolshevism, the other the defenders of civilization. Why is America in the wrong camp?" This was followed by news, comments on German culture and Living and the programs would frequently close with some Wagnerian music. They frequently referred to the American press as "Jewspapers". President Roosevelt was called "President Rosenfeldt". To gain more listeners they frequently gave out the names of captured Americans. After I was reported "missing" my parents listened nightly to the German programs hoping to hear that I was listed as a prisoner.

The International Red Cross maintained a partial surveillance of POW camps under German and Japanese control. A monthly bulletin was sent to service men's relatives. The Germans cooperated reasonably well and allowed Red Cross inspectors into the more established camps. All of the camps were alerted to upcoming visits and were "polished up" prior to their arrival. Men were ordered to shave, the guards often had newly pressed uniforms, some Red Cross food parcels were distributed, more potatoes were added to the soup, and the grounds cleaned up. In several camps additional blankets were issued to the POW's before the visits, only to be collected afterwards. POWs were "encouraged" to voice any complaints to the inspectors but were cautious in doing so since the inspectors would be gone in a day or two but the camp guard staff would still be around. The harsh conditions in some camps and the forced marches didn't really become apparent until after the camps were liberated.

## *Enlisted Men's Camp*

We were first housed in old stables that had now been converted into barracks. Each housed about 200 men. The floors were of cold concrete. Wooden bunks, three high, were covered with lice infested straw mattresses and we were each given one thin blanket. Two small coal stoves were placed in the center of each room. Since there was no fuel for them they weren't any help. Even though the stoves were not lighted men would still hover around them.

We spent most of our time huddled in our bunks trying to keep warm and picking out lice. In a few days I caught dysentery and pneumonia. I was removed to a sick ward where I stayed for about 5 days. A doctor, a Russian prisoner who held the rank of sergeant treated me. Opium tablets were the common medicine for treatment of dysentery. These seemed to work. The dysentery did return several times over the next few months, however. Then, since I wasn't strong enough for work details outside of the camp, I was assigned to work inside the camp.

According to the Geneva Convention, which the Germans did not always follow, enlisted men below the rank of sergeant were required to work, if needed, supposedly on non-military tasks. Sergeants could work if they wanted to and officers were not allowed to work at all. Also we were supposed to be paid 80 cents per day. The Germans interpreted this to mean 80 pfennigs per day. Since the German Mark was worth about 20 cents U.S. this meant that we would be paid at the rate of about 16 cents per day. However, considering the rate at which we worked and the quality of our work we were probably over paid at that. One German guard said the Americans were poor workers, they were always, "sitting, walking, talking, smoking, but not working. Scrip called "Kreigsgefanen Lager Gelt" or War Prisoners Camp Money was given to us periodically. This was supposedly redeemable at camp canteens. I never saw a POW canteen during my stay. Even if there were canteens there was probably nothing to buy.

My assignment was to work as an orderly to a recently opened officer compound, Oflag XIIIB. The term "Oflag." is short for "Officer Camp". The Germans believed that the officers should have a staff of orderlies to take care of their menial tasks. Therefore about 50 enlisted men were assigned to them.

This compound was set up for American officers just transferred from Poland. This group, numbering about 900, was forced marched from Poland and East Prussia to prevent their being rescued by the Russians. In this group was Colonel John Waters who was the son in law of General George Patton. More about him later. They told of considerable hardships suffered during their two-month march through the cold winter weather.

## *OFLAG. XIIIB*

The entire camp itself was quite large, housing prisoners of nearly every nationality. As I mentioned before, there were British, French, Russian, Italian, and Yugoslav sectors as well as the American enlisted men's compound. Altogether there must have been over five thousand prisoners in the camp. Of those about 3,500 were Americans. The Oflag XIIIB compound was a couple acres in area. One large two-story building housed the kitchen and sick ward. A few high-ranking officers were also housed there. Eight or nine buildings all originally built as troop barracks housed the other officers. The orderlies were housed in one building. There was a good-sized parade ground, called "Appel Plaz" in front of the two-story building. The latrine was at one end of the parade ground. A double barbed wire fence with guard towers surrounded the compound. Serb and Croatian compounds straddled the officer's area. The other nationalities were scattered around other parts of the camp.

The 900 officers who made the forced march were the "residents" of the compound. Some of these men, including Colonel Waters, were captured in North Africa. They, along with other officers captured on the ground in Italy, were marched and transported by train the length of Italy in a trek that took several months. As was the usual German custom, airmen were housed in separate camps called Stalag Luft for enlisted men, or Oflag Luft for officers. As the Russians advanced towards Germany these officers were forced marched across Germany to prevent them from being liberated. This group included seven full colonels, fifteen Lieutenant Colonels, many Majors, and Lieutenants. There were two Catholic and seven Protestant chaplains along with one Rabbi and five or six physicians. At this stage of the war the Germans did not show any hostility towards the American Jews at Hammelburg probably because they realized that the war would soon be over and it would not be in their best interest to antagonize their conquerors.

Once the group of orderlies took up residence we appointed a couple men to contact the highest-ranking American officer, Col. Goode, to define our responsibilities. At this point I would like to talk about some topics that would give a picture of what life was like in Hammelburg Lager.

## *Food Service*

My first job was to work in the camp kitchen tending fires and cleaning vegetables. This was considered to be a good job since the kitchen was warm. The kitchen was located in a building that was at one time part of an old German army hospital. The cooking equipment consisted of two enormous coal fired pressure cookers

76

(each about 5ft in diameter), which were used to prepare all of the camp meals. Other tasks to which the orderlies were assigned included carrying food, sweeping up the area, tending the sick ward, cleaning the latrine, and supporting the bi-weekly arrival of the "Scheisswagen" which cleaned out the latrines. More about this later.

Cooking for the camp was quite an experience. Into the cookers went potatoes, rutabagas, turnips, dehydrated vegetables, sugar beet pulp (after the sugar had been removed), and once a week a side of a cow or horse. Occasionally we were given soup made from dehydrated green vegetables, which occasionally contained worms, that was nicknamed "The Green Hornet Stew". No one was able to figure out what the vegetables were. The pressure cooker reduced nearly everything to a soup that was either thick or thin depending upon the potato ration for the week. Some of the rutabagas weighed as much as fifteen pounds and were able to resist all of the efforts of the pressure cooker. Considerable negotiation was required to obtain an axe from the Germans so that they could be cut up. The axe was delivered in the morning by a guard and collected by another guard in the evening.

One American doctor figured that our diet consisted of about 900 calories per day. Hunger was always on your mind. It took the form of a persistent ache in your stomach that was temporarily satisfied after each meal. After a few minutes however the ache was back. Some men considered catching the ever present rats and cooking them. The camp medical officer advised against this since the lice on the rats carried sicknesses. A few large black birds were caught and cooked. Report was that they were tough. Potatoes formed the basis of most of the soups. At first these were peeled since the Germans used human fertilizer to grow them. It was later decided that a good scrubbing would be better since it would reduce the amount of waste and preserved the most nourishing part of the potato, the peel. After an hour or so in the pressure they were reduced to a thin puree and I doubt that any germs could have survived the heat.

Typically we had two soups along with an eighth of a loaf of bread per day. In the morning we received a cup of "ersatz" coffee made from roasted barley. On the days when meat was included in the soup, only one meal was served. This wasn't much of a treat since one or two sides of a horse or cow didn't go very far with 900 men. To stretch the meat ration, the carcass was actually used three days. On the first day the carcass was cut into large chunks and boiled with the rest of the soup. Before serving, the meat was removed and held for the next day. On the second day the meat was then cut into small pieces and served in the soup. The pieces had to be small enough so that each of the 900 men got at least one bite. On the third day the bones were thrown into the soup to extract every last bit of food value.

Serving the food was done with considerable care. At mealtime orderlies were dispatched to the kitchen to pick up vats of soup allotments for each barracks. The officers then parceled out the soup to individuals. It looked strange to see colonels and majors arguing that they didn't receive the correct number of potatoes in their soup. In the orderlies barracks the procedure was as follows. The individual bowls were placed on a table anonymously. One man was assigned to ladle out the soup under the close supervision by all concerned. The ladeler filled his bowl last to make sure the portions were equal. This job was rotated among all the orderlies. Comments were made like "too much liquid in my bowl or you missed my piece of meat." The cutting of the bread loaves was also closely supervised. Each loaf was cut into eight equal pieces and again the man cutting the loaf had the last choice. On days when we received bits of margarine or jam the "accounting" became extra tight.

On two occasions Red Cross parcels were issued. These packages contained canned foods, biscuits, chocolate, powdered milk, and the all-important Domino brand cigarettes. The cigarettes became a form of currency. The Germans carefully removed all of the pepper from these packages since it could be used to ruin the guard dog's sense of smell. These packages were supposed to be allocated one per week to each prisoner. The two packages that were issued during my stay each had to be divided among six men. The Germans thoughtfully opened each tin can for us. This was done not out of consideration for our welfare, but to prevent the stock piling of food for escape. Powdered milk, under the brand name KLIM (milk spelled backwards) was also included in the packages. It took forever to dissolve it in water. The empty KLIM cans were often carefully fashioned into small stoves for brewing tea. To make the canned food more effective we combined our tinned rations with the regular soup.

To give you an idea to the extent that some food items were used, the Germans occasionally issued some prunes. Three or four men would group their allotment and carefully cook the prunes to soften them up. The liquid was either drunk or allowed to ferment which supposedly created a mild buzz. The cooked prunes were then eaten. The shells were opened to get at the nuts inside, which were also eaten. The remnants of the shells were then used as fuel for the KLIM stoves.

The Domino brand cigarettes included in the packages became the camp medium of exchange. A few of the men were so addicted to cigarettes that they traded away their food items for cigarettes. They were upset with me (I didn't smoke) because I withheld "selling" my cigarettes until their supplies dwindled and I got a better "price". I also gave some of them to patients in the hospital, which infuriated the addicted smokers even more.

As long as you were busy the lack of adequate food was not a top item on your mind. The evenings were long and dark since we only had one bare electric light bulb hanging from the ceiling, which did not provide adequate light for reading. This was turned off as nine P.M. After this time the only light came from the searchlight on one of the guard towers which periodically scanned the area. When the workday was over and men were sitting around swapping stories around the stove the subject of food would often surface. They would talk about favorite recipes and restaurants. This would go on for about an hour until someone would holler "Knock is off, let's change the subject!" At night, getting to sleep on an empty growling stomach was not easy.

## *Personal Behavior*

The way the men handled themselves as prisoners was an interesting study in human behavior. In addition to the careful review of the food allocation other personality traits developed. The evening discussions were almost entirely devoted to home life prior to their army service. One man was badly "shell shocked" and did not speak at all. It was an unwritten rule that we would not steal from each other. Stealing from the Germans was O.K. There were the usual wheeler-dealers trying to bargain for more food or smokes. Tempers flared occasionally but no serious fights erupted. Some men had to be forced to keep clean. Fortunately the weather was cold and we didn't smell too bad.

Keeping clean was a real problem. I received only two warm showers in four months. Other bathing was done using a bucket of cold water and a rag. If you tried to dry the rag outside after washing it would freeze. Soap was in short supply. When I worked in the hospital I managed to "funnel" some soap from the hospital into the orderlies since the hospital had a good supply. Because we had only one set of underwear, if we were lucky, this was washed over and over again until it was in shreds. Working in the hospital allowed me

81

to use a bit of hot water for washing. This was a mixed blessing for when my injured foot and knee got too warm they ached.

Keeping the lice under control was nearly impossible. When we took our rare showers our clothes were deloused with powder. This didn't help much since our mattresses were filled with lice. Pet names were given for three categories of lice. These were named after categories of German soldiers. The first was the Volksturm (peoples army) louse, which would run across your body but would not bite. The second was the Wehrmach (regular army) louse that would maneuver and then bite. The worst were the S.S. lice! They would creep slowly so as to not be observed and then bite hard. For an evening's entertainment we would pick the lice from our clothing and drop them onto the top of the stove and watch them sizzle.

## *Black Troops*

About a dozen orderlies were black. These men, captured in North Africa, were from the 333$^{rd}$ Field Artillery Battalion, 155 mm heavy artillery. This unit was comprised of black troops led by white officers. Integration had not yet become standard practice in the armed forces. This battalion had the reputation of being the best artillery battalion in Europe and Africa. Their battle cry was "Rommel, count your men", (the lanyard was then pulled), "how many have you got now?" In our group there was no race hostility, in fact a black sergeant named Theo Johnson, from Palm Beach Florida, was named our leader even though other white sergeants outranked him. While I worked at the hospital he daily saw to it that I always received my correct food ration by handing it to me through the barbed wire fence. On outside work details the guards, especially the younger ones were intimidated by the black men. Various stories had been passed around through the German army circles such as "the blacks were savages recruited from Africa to bolster weak American forces!" One large black man took great delight in intimidating the younger guards assigned to outside camp details by just staring at them. Some of them would come completely apart.

## *Religious Services*

As I mentioned before there was no shortage of chaplains. The two catholic chaplains, Father Madden and Father Cavanaugh held Mass in both the officer and enlisted compounds. The Protestant chaplains also held services in both compounds. The Germans were cooperative with the chaplains and procured religious items from the local churches so services could be held. Prior to his enlistment in the army, Fr. Cavanaugh was an instructor at Loyola University in Chicago. Even the Rabbi was provided with materials! Just how this was accomplished was never explained.

## *Diversions*

Aside from the drill sessions and ball games, there were some activities that did help to relieve the tension of being confined. What few decks of cards that were available were worn, dog-eared and "marked." The few books that were available were also worn and tattered. Typical extra diversions were the following.

## *Goose-Step*

Each morning at about eight o'clock the entire camp, officers and orderlies, would fall out in the "Appelplaz (assembly area) for roll call or "appel" in German. Each group of fifty men would be counted. The guards would make trips to the latrine to check on who was there. With dysentery so prevalent there was always one or two men in the latrine. Afterwards, we performed about one half hour of close order drill to keep limber.

One morning the orderlies fell out into ranks to be counted as usual. After the routine count and checks of the latrine by two German soldiers, the orderly "platoon" decided to do a demonstration of Nazi goose-step marching for the reviewing German sergeant. A POW sergeant shouted some commands and we proceeded to Goose-Step around the parade ground passed the officers and the reviewing German sergeant. We gave him a raised arm "Hitler" salute. He watched with amusement. When we were through he called the two German privates to attention. After a few commands the trio Goosed-Stepped off of the parade ground showing how it was really done. We were rank amateurs compared to them. The entire company of officers and enlisted orderlies applauded them.

## *"Feur Man, Scheisswagen"*

About twice a week we were treated to the arrival of the "Scheisswagen," a vehicle used to pump out the latrine. "Scheiss (or Scheisz) wagen" literally means "Shit wagon." The latrine consisted of an open pit covered with a box like structure with several roughly 10 inch diameter holes placed on top to allow one to do one's business. The name "Feur Man" was given to the old German soldier who accompanied the vehicle. He always asked a detail of "Feur Man, (four men) Scheisswagen" to assist the pumping process. I won't go into the details of what had to be done to support this operation. As one can imagine this was not the most desirable job in the camp. To be fair the duty was rotated among the orderlies. The entire camp generally fell out for the arrival of the Scheisewagen.

The "Scheisswagen" was truly a marvel of Germanic engineering. The pumper was mounted on a one and one half-ton truck powered by gas produced by a smelly charcoal-burning generator. The pump consisted of a large tank, about 4 ft. in diameter and 10 ft. long, with a 3 ft. diameter riser about 2 ft. high in the center. It looked somewhat like a railroad tank car. On top of the riser was a large rubber flapper valve. A large hose about 8 inches in diameter ran from the top of tank into one of the openings in the latrine. It was the job of one orderly to keep the hose submerged in the latrine sump. The tank operator lifted up a corner of the flapper valve and poured in a small amount of fluid, probably gasoline, from a glass bottle. He then closed the valve, stepped aside and pressed a button on the side. A huge flame leaped out of the top of the riser forcing open the valve. When the valve closed it created a partial vacuum in the tank. With a large sucking noise the contents of the latrine were pumped into the tank. This operation was repeated several times as needed. This was often accompanied by applause from the troops. The truck then motored off to a nearby farm where is contents was distributed. The detail then reassembled the latrine floorboards and the audience disbursed.

## *Hospital Assignment*

After a week in the kitchen I was assigned to work as an orderly in a sick ward in an adjacent hospital compound which was staffed by Serbian doctors. My job was to take care of a ward used for treating seriously ill American patients. The ward contained 12 to 14 beds that were always occupied. The cases included pneumonia, dysentery, jaundice, bomb and combat injuries with infections, and other serious cases. During my four-week stay four men died of various causes. Three died in one night. My job was to keep the ward clean, tend the fires, make beds, empty bedpans, and change bandages; give shots, wash patients and serve food. The workday began at about 7:00 am and ended at about 9:00 PM with frequent calls during the night to empty bedpans or urine bottles "dead ducks". Even though the days were long and hard the work made the time pass quickly. A German guard named Ostertag daily inspected the ward and instructed me as to what work needed to be done. The Serbian doctors were very skillful and dedicated and did remarkable work with the limited resources available, such as bandages made of paper. Live maggots were used to eat away decayed flesh to limit infection in open wounds. Watching this activity took some effort. American doctors from the officer's compound made frequent visits to check up on treatment and were impressed with what the Serbs did with the limited resources. Being a hospital orderly I was allowed to visit other sick wards in the camp in order to obtain supplies. One afternoon during the week I became a "dental assistant" to a Serbian dentist. My job was to operate the foot-actuated drill while he ground away on patient's teeth. I also had to clean up. No novocaine was available for dental work and filling and extracting teeth was quite painful. During one session the dentist worked on a bridge for his own mouth. He ground away on his teeth using a mirror in front of him. Occasionally a Serbian Colonel named Yovachich (sp?) brought news of the war via a radio smuggled into the British sector.

Several of the Serbs would come into the ward to get help in studying English. One Serb, named Rasha, was especially kind and helped us get additional supplies from the Germans. I spent several hours helping him to improve his English. One day he said that the didn't know what would happen when the war was over since the Communists would most likely be in power in his country and they would not be too considerate of those of the old regime.

The hospital doctors came from a compound housing about 200 Serbian prisoners adjacent to the American officer sector. On the other side of officer sector was a compound housing a similar number of Croatian prisoners. One would think that since they were both Yugoslavs that they would get along. Nothing could be further from the truth. Prior to their capture, the Croatians were for the Communists and the Serbs were for the old aristocracy of Yugoslavia and the two groups didn't get along together at all! The only thins they had in common was their hatred of the Germans. One day each week the gates from the two compounds would be opened and groups of men were allowed to travel under guard across the American compound from one sector to the other to visit friends or relatives. Things were usually peaceful for about an hour until someone would start talking politics. Fights would break out and upon one occasion the fighting was so widespread the Germans brought in a fire truck and hosed down the whole group. Soaking wet the prisoners then returned to their respective compounds and geared up for the next confrontation.

## *Outside Camp Work Details*

After four weeks in the hospital another American POW was given my job since he was trained as a combat medic and I wasn't. By this time I had regained some of my health, even though I weighed only about 110 pounds and I was transferred to work details outside the camp. Things now definitely became more exciting. Early in the war these optional details, Arbiets Kommando, were voluntary and desirable since the food was generally better. Now that things were becoming desperate for the Germans, work detail were not optional.

Earlier in my stay we all were told that trying to escape from a work detail outside the camp was definitely inadvisable because if you were caught you were shot! Later on this philosophy was applied to all escape attempts. To get the point across, one morning after roll call we were not dismissed as usual but told to stay in ranks. While we waited, a horse drawn cart was brought into the appelplatz. The cart contained the bodies of four American soldiers who tried to escape from a work detail and were caught and executed. The horse was unhitched and led away. We then were told to remain in ranks throughout the morning. Additional guards were posted to assure our undivided attention. One by one, men were allowed to go to the latrine. Sometime after noon the horse was re-hitched to the wagon and the bodies hauled away. We were then dismissed without comment from the camp Commandant. The point was well made!

The first group to which I was assigned was transported by truck to the town of Germunden where we (about 25 of us) were put to work repairing railroad tracks through the town. Working on the German railroads at this time was very dangerous because of frequent air attacks. The words "Amerikanischer Flugzeug" along with the air raid sirens quickly got one's attention. American and British fighter aircraft, after escorting bombers to their targets, would often hedge-hop along the railroad tracks on their way back home and shoot up trains and track repair crews. I was strafed several times during my three-week tour. The US P-51 Mustang fighter was much feared by prisoners since it was very quiet and they were often over and gone before you were aware of their presence. The P-47 Thunderbolts and the P-38 Lightnings were quite loud and often gave ample warning. We were very fortunate in that during the three weeks tour our crew was together, only four men were wounded and no one was killed. During one such attack I dove into a ditch only to have a guard land on top of me knocking my wind out. After the planes passed he then pointed to the planes and said, "diener comarade" (your friends). I replied, "not now!" On another attack the strafing planes caused a locomotive boiler to explode, scalding the German engineer. Four American prisoners pulled him from the cab and kept him from receiving serious burns.

Because of the frequent strafing attacks most train travel took place at night. Trains were often protected by "flak" cars fitted with twin 40 mm anti-aircraft guns. These cars followed the locomotive and tender and occasionally they were attached to the end of the train. How effective they were I couldn't say. They were, however, quite loud. Most of the trains I saw were freight carriers. I did see one train of boxcars carrying civilians parked on a siding. The doors were open and people milled around. Since there were no guards I imagine that these people were refugees being relocated away from the front lines.

We encountered prisoners of several nationalities, Russians being the most common. Russians, both military and civilians, were conscripted by the Germans to perform a variety of tasks. These ranged from railroad work, removing bomb wreckage to building reconstruction. Many Russian prisoners were actually better off in Germany than they were under the Stalin regime. When Germany surrendered many of these men were executed when they returned home for collaborating with the Germans.

On one-track repair detail we encountered a group of mostly French prisoners. One of these men wore an American uniform. When I tried to talk to him he didn't understand me. It turned out that he was a Belgian farmer who had stolen an American army uniform and was then caught up by the Germans in the battle of the Bulge. They couldn't understand him so they sent him back as a prisoner. By the time they found out that he was a civilian he was too far into Germany to be sent home so they just put him to work. The civilians in the towns, at this time, did not display open hostility to working prisoners. The Germans maintained checkpoints where identity papers of both civilians and military were carefully examined. Any persons without proper papers were promptly arrested.

During the nights we were locked up in vacant buildings in the towns where we were put to work. British bombing raids often kept us awake. It was often difficult to determine just how close the blasts were. Long after the war I told a British marketing representative of company near London that I did not remember what the top-side of a Lancaster bomber looked like since all I saw was the bottom. He thoughtfully sent me a large photo of the topside of one. Not being able to see what was going on while locked in the room at night was quite unnerving. The air raid sirens had three warning patterns. When enemy aircraft were in the area three five second blasts were given. If an attack was imminent, fifteen short blasts were given. One long blast, of about ten seconds, sounded the "all-clear". In the mornings when we were released we were each given a piece of bread with some jam or margarine and a cup of "Ersatz" coffee. Then we were either marched or trucked to our next job site. One morning en route to our work site we passed the body of a German soldier hanging from a tree with a sign reading "Deserteur" deserter in German.

One afternoon a group of about ten of us was taken by truck to another town where an unexploded American bomb had landed on the railroad track. We were then told to remove it! We were not too enthusiastic about removing it since bombs, even duds, often had the nasty habit of exploding when they were moved. Even our guard who, was probably in his late 60's, was wary of this task. The olive drab bomb sat there, scratched, dented, fins bent seemingly daring someone to move it. You could read something like "High explosive, 500 lbs, Rockford Arsenal, batch number, contract date." etc. We searched for boards to pry it up, all the time stalling as much as we could. Finally it got too dark and the relieved guard took us back to our billet. We were fortunate that our guard was old. The older guards were generally more understanding. The young guards, often 16 or 17 year- old kids were very unpredictable and inclined to shoot. The next morning the bomb was gone probably removed by some nearby

92

Russians. While shoveling bomb wreckage in the towns, the civilians generally ignored us. Throughout the war year's prisoners of nearly all nationalities worked in the towns and farms all over Germany.

## *Return to Camp*

For about three days our crew along with two or three others labored to replace a section of track through the ruined railroad yards in the town of Wurtzburg. The night following completion of the line a British air raid destroyed what we had done and we were sent back to camp. I was treated for shock, resulting from bomb blasts at a hospital in a castle near the city before being returned. I was again put to work as an orderly in the same Serbian hospital from which I left. Ostertag greeted me and put me to work. He was a jovial sort but wouldn't put up with any crap. He was an old soldier who had fought on many fronts. His uniform bore the Crimea patch, the Afrika Corps badge and other battle insignia. He had been wounded and sent back to guard prisoners. Since I grew up in a Jewish neighborhood of Chicago I managed to learn quite a bit of Yiddish which is actually a dialect of German. I talked to Ostertag as well as I could in a mixture of English, German and Yiddish. In one conversation he told of his experiences fighting the various armies. He said the French were not interested in fighting, the Italians were disorganized, the British fought furiously in the morning but stopped in the afternoon "for Tea", and the Russians kept coming, and coming, and coming, and

93

coming. He said that what the Americans lacked in strategy they made up with ammunition!

One afternoon a German army captain entered the ward and asked in American accented English if there was anyone here from Chicago. I answered that I was. He then said that he had a brother who owned a meat market in Chicago whom he had not seen in years. He said that he knew the war would be over soon and that I would probably be home before he was and asked if I would contact his brother and tell him that he was still alive. I wrote down his brother's name and thought nothing more of it until I was on home on leave. I expand upon this later.

In early March it was obvious that the war was nearing an end. At night you could hear the rumble of guns at the front, some 50 or 60 miles away. Even with this, most of us didn't think the war would be over until mid summer. Some of the men got seeds from the Germans and planted gardens. Father Cavanaugh, a Catholic Chaplain captured with the 106th Division was planning an Easter service, which he said that "God willing we won't be here to attend". As a result of the following action he got his wish, but it was not how he had planned.

## *The Baum Raid. Freedom?*

On about March 25th we were suddenly locked down and the Germans put all of the Americans (officers and enlisted men) on alert to be prepared to move to another camp. We had no idea as to what was going on. The men spent the day gathering what few personal effects they had. I was put to work getting the ambulatory hospital patients ready to be moved. After this I was then sent back to the orderly barracks. On the afternoon of March 26 we heard gunfire near the camp. Rumors quickly spread that the army had broken through to liberate us. Later the guards disappeared and shortly afterwards the gunfire became very close. A nearby storage building was set afire. About 4PM a column of tanks and armored personnel carriers, about 300 men, from the U.S. Fourth Armored Division of General Patton's army, rolled into the compound over the barbed wire fences. There was an incredible feeling of exhilaration over the belief that we were being freed! This feeling quickly evaporated, however, when we learned that this was a rescue column sent to recover only certain American officers.

This episode, known as the Baum raid, (named after Captain Baum, the commander of the column) was quite controversial since one of the officers they were sent to recover was General Patton's son-in-law, Lt. Col. Waters. Lt.Col. Waters had been captured in Tunisia and marched the length of Italy and was eventually transported by train to a prison camp in East Prussia. He was then forced marched, along with the 900 other American officers mentioned above, to Hammelburg. General Patton was criticized for the operation and later denied that the mission was implemented to rescue him alone. Patton denied that he knew Waters was at Hammelbug. He could have guessed that Waters was in Oflag XIIIB since the Germans notified the Red Cross that the officer's camp in

East Prussia where he was housed was being evacuated. The Red Cross was also notified that a large number of American prisoners arrived in Hemmelburg in February. One of the tank commanders specifically asked for Lt.Col. Waters by name. During a skirmish when the tanks first arrived Colonel Waters was shot in the thigh by a guard and was left behind in the hospital.

Once the key officers were assembled the column started to leave. When we realized that this was only a limited rescue mission we had the option of staying behind or trying to make a break for it. Since there was some 60 miles of hostile German territory between the camp and the US lines and all of us were undernourished, the opportunity to try and escape wasn't very attractive. Some men took off on heir own but most of the prisoners returned to camp and waited for the guards to return. I managed to climb onto a tank, along with about 10 others, and rode out on it for a while. Other prisoners crowded onto other vehicles in the hope of making it back to our lines. It was now dark and it was an eerie feeling traveling through the darkened still towns. Even though this was the end of March it was still cold and bleak and there is nothing colder than the armor of a tank in winter. This trip lasted several hours. Passing through one small town, I believe that it was Hollirich, the column encountered stiff resistance from both heavy and small arms fire and the POW's were ordered off the tanks since we were hampering their operation. A small group of us ran back along the column and hid in a ditch until the shooting ceased. Since the tanks had now moved on, several of us started walking westward along a railroad track, not knowing where we were going. Very early the next morning a few of us met up with the US armored column which now contained a number of liberated officers including Col. Goode, the highest ranking officer in the camp.

To prevent the return of the column to the U.S. lines the Germans had blown up a bridge, forcing the column to return by another route. A few of us again climbed aboard the tanks and rode out to a hilltop clearing in a forested area. By this time nearly three-quarters of the initial column vehicles had been lost. The remaining tanks and half-tracks were grouped together in a small clearing next to a barn. Fuel was running low and several vehicles were being abandoned. Also, about 10 wounded men were off-loaded and placed in the barn in the hope that the Germans would take care of them. A red marker was then placed on one side of the barn. At dawn after the wounded had been moved and fuel transferred to a few undamaged vehicles, the column got ready to move out. Shortly after the tanks were started, two German light tanks and a platoon of infantrymen, which had moved up unobserved, opened fire on the group. The men hopped out of the vehicles and headed for the barn. The half-track in which I was riding was hit and its gasoline tanks exploded. One of my fellow prisoners yanked me off the vehicle and we both ran towards the barn. I got off with burns on my arm and hands and laid down next to the barn with the other men. While pinned down, several men of the rescue party threw away their captured German souvenir pistols. It was only a matter of minutes before a white flag, someone's undershirt, was displayed, and we all surrendered. Again I stood around with my hands on top of my head.

## *Captured Again.*

The Germans searched the surrounding woods for escapees. They then transported us back to Hammelburg camp by trucks where the wounded were separated from the others. In the ambush, in addition to the burns I received, the sores on my foot opened up. Unable to walk I was included in the hospitalized group. After the raid, the Germans rounded up as many of the escaped prisoners as possible and prepared to evacuate the Americans from the camp. The American prisoners, numbering over 3,000 (both officers and enlisted men) were marched out of the camp eastward in the direction of Ragensburg. Prisoners of other nationalities were left behind under guard in the camp. The Americans were kept on the road for nearly a month before being liberated. The Germans had planned to use the prisoners as bargaining tools should things get rough. The 14th Armored Division of the Seventh Army finally freed the group of wounded and sick Americans, numbering about 75, left behind at Hammelburg, on April 9th. While hospitalized I again suffered from dysentery and my weight dropped to less than 100 lbs. When it comes to rapid weight reduction, dysentery will put all of the major diet weight reduction plans to shame!

The feeling of exhilaration at being finally freed was at first subdued, since two weeks before we had gone through a very painful false alarm. When we realized that this was indeed the real thing, our joy was hard to contain.

Since Oflag XIIIB and Stalag XIII C were among the first German prison camps to be liberated by the Americans, the troops were not experienced at handling suddenly freed prisoners. Along with the sick and injured Americans at Hammelburg there were still several thousand Russians, French, British, Yugoslavs, and Italians, many of whom had been prisoners for as long as five years. When the gates were opened many of these men went into towns and farms and stole food and anything in sight. A herd of sheep that had been grazing on a hillside near the camp disappeared in a matter of a few hours. German civilians were ready targets for the rage that had been built up during years of miserable prison treatment and several were beaten and killed. After a couple of days the US troops realized their mistake and they rounded up the prisoners and placed them under control. Our first meal of Army food made most of us quite ill since we were not used to rich food. The doctors then modified our diet to ease our systems back to normalcy. The liberating American troops who visited the sick and injured were appalled at our condition.

## *The Trip Home*

After the euphoria of being liberated began to wear off, preparations were made to transport all sick and wounded to hospitals in France. It took about three or four days before I was well enough to make the trip.

When ready, we were assembled outside the sick ward in preparation for departure, I looked around at the buildings and other prisoners still awaiting transfer. I actually felt a tinge of nostalgia for this cold, miserable place. After sharing experiences with other people under these unpleasant conditions I felt a bond with them. I even felt sorry for some of the guards now that their country was ruined. Ostertag, dressed in a clean uniform and wearing a Red Cross armband, said good bye and wished me well and I wished him the same. I waved to the Serbs in the next compound and wondered what would happen to them if they were sent home to the Communists. After the war many of these men were forcefully repatriated only to be killed by the Communists, a dismal end after suffering for over four years under the Germans.

An Army Ambulance took me to the airfield at Darmstadt where I boarded a C-47 for the trip to a hospital near Epinal, France. The flight was uncomfortable since I didn't have much meat on my backside and the bucket seats were not padded. There was also some turbulence. I remember passing over the ruins of Frankfurt and wondered if all of Germany looked like this. When we arrived at an airfield near Epinal, we were transferred to a hospital, which was set up in an old five or six story French resort hotel. Every thing about it was "vintage" including the iron cage elevator that would not go past the fourth floor if it contained more than two people.

The hospital was filled with combat casualties and sick patients. The group I was in, about 20, was the first group of ex-prisoners admitted to the hospital. We were a sorry looking bunch! Our hair was long, we were unshaven and all were very thin. When I was lifted onto a bed a nurse was shocked to see that she could put her thumb and forefinger around my leg I was so thin! I could do the same near my thigh. The hospital orderly then shaved off all of my hair to get rid of any lice and other creatures. I was given a blood transfusion and slowly acclimated to army food. I was able to walk around after a couple of days and spent time with the other G.I.s swapping stories. My fellow liberated prisoners were all thriving and anxious to get home. A recovering British POW, with a sense of humor, described his long term of captivity as comprising of "frequent daily walks through the countryside, (i.e. 30 mile daily forced marches), nightly camp-outs under the stars, (on the ground in freezing weather), comprehensive diet designed to keep us trim, (starvation diet), closely supervised on-the-job training, (shoveling bomb wreckage under heavy guard), occasional delousing, (which only made the lice grow faster), nightly fireworks displays, (RAF bombing raids), and exhilarating jogs down railroad tracks (spurred on by American fighter planes strafing the repair crews),

The Red Cross sent a telegram to my parents telling of my release. It turned out that they had received a post card in late March, which I had mailed shortly after I was captured saying that I was a prisoner.

Since the hospital was filled to overflowing with combat casualties the staff wanted to make room for new patients. There were a large number of men who had recovered but were feigning illness to keep from going back to the front. It was spring the weather was turning warm and the countryside was becoming green again. This was the first time that I appreciated that Europe could actually look nice. When I landed in Europe in October, the leaves had already fallen and the countryside was bleak and cold. This impression continued throughout what was one of the coldest European winters on record. To this day my impressions of Europe during my tour are all black, or gray except for fires. I have very little memory of color.

The nice weather made some of the patients antsy for exercise. To weed out the men who were now fit to return to the front, a senior hospital staff member proposed that a baseball game be held featuring "hospital personnel vs. patients". This brought out a large number of men who were eagerly looking forward to a good game. While the game was in progress, doctors scanned the patient team with binoculars from the hospital windows and identified the most active.

These men were then reviewed, marked for duty and most were sent back to the front!

After about two weeks I was still thin but much better. I was released and given orders to report to staging camp near Le. Havre named "Camp Lucky Strike". Two other such camps were also named after cigarettes, Camel and Philip Morris. I was taken by truck to Paris where I checked into a RAMP camp. This stood for "Recovered Allied Military Personnel." There I was given a place to sleep, a new uniform and a cash advance of U.S./ French invasion currency.

Paris was a marvelous city even after the hardships suffered under the Germans for over five years. The traffic was chaotic and the sidewalks were filled with natives, as well as G.I.'s. I took the usual sightseeing trips, had lunch or coffee in the sidewalk café's. I wondered if I was eating or drinking in the same spots my father visited as a Beaux-Arts student in 1912. There also pretty girls walking along the sidewalks, phenomena I hadn't been exposed to since I left England eight months before. I spent two Days in Paris and then took a train from the "Gare de L'EST" station and headed for Le Havre. The passenger compartment, in which I was riding, had patched-up bullet holes in the compartment wall probably put there by strafing American fighter aircraft.

The city of Le Havre was still a mess but it was much better than it was six months before. The camp was a few miles out of town and was nothing more than a huge array of drab eight man tents.

There wasn't much to do other than eat and play cards. I avoided the card games based upon previous experience.

On May 9, two days after my arrival, the end of the war was announced. There was much celebrating and since beer and wine was readily available there were a lot of drunken men. That evening there was a scary display of captured weapons. The night was filled with gunfire from souvenir rifles, pistols and even machine pistols! The next day there was a shakedown of the camp to weed out banned weapons and ammunition. Souvenirs such as pistols and rifles were O.K. But some of the things recovered were live grenades, machine pistols, live Teller mines, rocket launchers, tons of ammunition and lord knows what. All of these things were confiscated since they were on the no-no souvenir list!

## *Atlantic Crossing*

Two days later I was assigned to a group of about 350 men who were transported to Le Havre harbor and loaded on board the Charles W. Acock for the trip to the States. This was a Victory ship that was being rotated back to the States probably for scrapping. We troops were quartered in the forward section of the ship. The bunks, were again the typical metal frame type with canvas covers stacked four high. I got number three berth this time. We spent most of the day cleaning up the mess left by the previous passengers.

After a day in port we set out through the same harbor opening through which I passed some nine months before. The "Anchoren

Verboten" sign had now been removed. When I made the trip into LeHavre in the year 2001 on a cruise ship the entrance through the breakwater looked the same. Everything else was much different. It brought back memories. We first sailed across the channel to a point outside the port of Southampton. There we waited for a couple of days while other ships were assembled into a convoy. Altogether, over 100 ships were grouped into our convoy. True, the war was officially over, but there was concern that some of the U-Boats had not yet gotten the word to surrender.

Once the group was organized we set sail for New York. We had no idea that the trip would take 25 days! The final assembly of the convoy took place out to sea off the coast of Ireland. As far as I could see there were ships. Some were damaged and were being towed home. Our ship was unladen except for the troops and had just enough ballast to keep it upright. This meant that the ship rocked and rolled at the least provocation. A few days out to sea we encountered about five days of moderately rough weather. The ship pitched up and down like a cork with the swells. Being relatively unloaded, the propeller would lift out of the water when the nose of the ship pitched downward, after the crest of a wave. This would produce a strong shaking motion in the ship for about 5 seconds followed by another five seconds of quiet after which the propeller dipped back into the water. This went on for four or five days! Needless to say there were many seasick men on board. While my stomach was queasy at times I didn't get sick.

The food service was good but far from gourmet status. We did get three meals per day (or six as some would put it, three down and three up). We had canned chicken and dehydrated potatoes for nearly every meal except breakfast. For breakfast we had dry milk and powdered eggs and until most of us couldn't stand them. Powdered eggs had the tendency to make one "fart". In a compartment filled with some 350 men this often produced some loud "musical" occasions. I was now putting on more weight and aside from the boredom I felt really very good. Like most of the other men I spent time reading or B.S-ing with the other men about experiences and home. While no one was officially in command we grouped together to get as much organized exercise as we could. There was the familiar bullhorn announcement "Army sweeping crews, man your brooms. Clean sweep down fore and aft." Again we were blessed with salt-water showers and the accompanying itching.

## *Home*

We arrived at New York harbor in the morning of June 6. The scene couldn't have been more spectacular! The sky was bright; spouting fireboats greeted the several troop ships with us. As we sailed past the Statue of Liberty many men who were seasoned combat veterans actually cried. After a long wait, we were nudged onto a pier by two tugboats. An Army band played popular songs and we were greeted by Red Cross girls handing out fresh milk! This was the first milk I had since I left for Europe. One would think that the experience of having a glass of milk would not be so significant. But not having had fresh milk since we left, to most of us this meant that we were really home. Being able to stand on firm ground was also a relief.

We were sent to Camp Kilmer for processing and reassignment. Former prisoners were each given a two-month leave before reporting to our next station. At this time I didn't know that the Division to which I was being assigned was to be trained for the invasion of Japan. After Europe I don't think I could have survived that.

After another long train ride I was once again home. I was shocked to see my mother now with all gray hair! I can't imagine how they felt, not knowing where I was after I was reported missing. Pop's spirits were bolstered somewhat when he won the Chicago Tribune "Theatre of the Air" architecture competition. The prize was $5,000 which was most welcome after losing so much during the stock market crash of 1929. I think that for the first two days at home I didn't do much more than sleep and unwind. Mom, at this time was working for the Army map service in Chicago, drawing contour maps. Being an artist this was an ideal job for her.

Again there was much time to renew old acquaintances and mourn the combat deaths of four of my high school friends. Bud filled me in on all of the latest rumors and news and we double dated. Harry was back from the Air Force as well as Dick. I did a little radio repair work but this dried up after the backlog was taken care of. I spent a few weeks working in the neighborhood bookie (horse betting parlor) chalking the board and cleaning up. The pay was $1.50 per hour plus bail!

Chicago was still the great service persons town it was during my last trip home. On night I double dated with a friend who was also home on leave. We were both in uniform and took our dates to the fancy Edgewater Beach Hotel Ballroom for dinner and dancing. We were trying to impress our dates but at the same time trying to keep costs down. When we asked the waiter for our check we were told that a guest had taken care of it. This happened a couple of more times during my leave.

Earlier in this story I mentioned the visit of a German Army Captain to my hospital ward in Oflag XIIIB. I remember him saying that he had a brother in Chicago who owned a meat market. I had his brother's name and looked for it in the phone directory. I found a similar name on an advertisement for a delicatessen on West Belmont Avenue. Still in uniform I took a streetcar out to the address. It was a typical neighborhood delicatessen filled with hanging sausages, barrels of pickles, semi-exotic foods and richly smelling of garlic. I approached a middle-aged woman (everyone over 30 looked middle aged to me) behind the counter. She asked, "What do you want?" I asked if Mr. Lowmeyer (I am not sure what his name really was) was there because I have a message from his brother. She went in back and returned with a man who looked much like the German officer. He then asked me to repeat what I said. I told him that I met his brother, a German army officer in a German prison camp last April. His face turned white and he looked as if he was going into shock. He then asked me to come into the back room where he poured a stiff drink for himself and gave me a bottle of beer. Then the following story then unfolded.

It seems that his parents, along with he and his brother, immigrated to the United States in the late 1920's from Germany. In the-mid 1930's his mother took the two boys back to Germany to visit relatives. She and one son returned in 1938 while the other son, now about 19, stayed behind for a longer visit. Since he was of German descent, even though he was a U.S. citizen, he was conscripted into the German army. The message I brought was the first that he had heard of his brother in over four years. When I left the delicatessen he loaded me down with sausages, cheeses and other foods to the point where I could hardly carry them. At Christmas time he sent my parents more food. About a year later his brother was released and allowed to return to America. I was invited to his coming home party, a large affair, where I was warmly greeted!

Once my leave was over I boarded a train for an R and R center in Miami Beach, Florida. This was to be a one-week Army sponsored rest program before joining my next division for training. Resting on the beach and enjoying the warm water was great. The nightlife was good and varied with many nightspots spread along the hotel area. . A sign above the bar in one tavern read, "All Army Air Force Colonels under 21 must be accompanied by their parents!" I took a trip to Daytona Beach where I lived for three years as a child. Daytona Beach was much the same as I had remembered, Fortunately, while I was in Miami the Japanese surrendered, ending all hostilities. There was wild celebrating in Miami even though all the bars and liquor stores were ordered closed. The next day a parade was held down Collins Avenue in Miami Beach, which included nearly all of the service people in town. It was a mixture of women and men from nearly every branch of service, grouped together in a random manner. Crowds lined the avenue and applauded and cheered as we paraded by. Despite the disorganized appearance of the group it was a wonderful experience. Shortly afterward I was presented with a Purple Heart for injuries suffered in December 1944.

## *Camp Crowder, Missouri*

Camp Crowder was another "cookie cutter" copy of typical army camps set up during the war. It was just outside Neosho, Missouri and about an hour from Joplin, Mo. The Division was to be trained for the invasion of Japan. Now that the war was over it seemed that the Division Commander didn't know what to do with us. Most of the time we just sat around and played pool. Several of us ex-prisoners objected to the fact that the German POW's had full reign of the clubs and PX while black American soldiers were confined to their own clubs. The Germans were then confined to their own areas.

Neosho was a typical Midwestern small town near a large army post. There were many bars and small restaurants, none of which was any good. While sitting at the bar in one saloon, (no one was worried about drinking age at this time); I noticed a large poster above the back-bar. It read, "Next Week is Bob Will's Week." I made the mistake of asking "So who is Bob Wills?" That nearly got me ousted. It seemed that Bob Wills was the leader of a well-known Country Band called "Bob Wills and his Texas Playboys". Bob Wills was born in Neosho and he was coming back for a series of homecoming performances.

One weekend I took a trip to Kansas City and visited my cousins. Bob and Bill Markey were home on leave and we swapped many stories. Cousins Margie and Betty Markey were there and we had a ball. Betty was about my age and a very pretty young woman. In a letter home I commented to my parents that it was shame that she was a cousin!

If one was adventurous you could go to the big city of Joplin, Missouri about an hour away. It too was filled with soldiers on weekend passes but was larger and able to handle them. I once read a column filler article in a Chicago newspaper datelined Joplin, Missouri that read, "A man on horseback was arrested for drunken driving. It turned out that he was sober but the horse was drunk!"

## *Fort Knox, Kentucky*

Fort Knox was the last stop in my military career. Now that Japan had capitulated there was no need to train the division at Camp

Crowder for an invasion. We idled our time away for a few weeks thinking that we were probably slated for the army of occupation.

In early October the decision was made to break up the contingent at Camp Crowder and reassign its personnel. I received orders to report to Fort Knox, Kentucky. There I was posted to a Military Police company. I was issued M.P. equipment and waited for assignment. On one weekend I was paired with another green M.P. who was about 6 ft. 5 ins. and assigned to town patrol. We must have looked like something out of a comic strip, me at about 5 ft. 8 ins. and him at 6 ft. 5 ins.!

Our duty post was one of the roughest spots in Louisville. With Fort Knox so close to Louisville it was crawling with G.I.s (sometimes literally crawling) especially on the weekends. We pulled the 4 PM. to midnight shift in a neighborhood filled with sleazy bars. Along with our white helmets and M.P. armbands we were each given an enormous 45 Caliber Colt revolver, without any ammunition, and a Billy club. With these we were to maintain law and order!

The biggest problem we faced was drunks passing out on the sidewalks. We also received a ration of crap because of the comical look we presented. Fortunately all we did handle that night were a couple of passed out drunks. These were loaded into M.P. wagons and taken back to camp.

. Once this session was over I decided to see if there were any other jobs available that were more filling of my "talents". The post stockade indicated that they had an opening for a clerk-typist. This sounded right up my alley since I knew how to type. I was accepted and then settled into a rather comfortable job. My shift extended from 7 am. until. 1 PM with the rest of the day off.

My job was to process incoming prisoners, mostly drunks and AWOL's, and type up the daily report. I also had to screen outgoing mail. It was unbelievable the problems many of these men got themselves into. Since I was now held the rank of Corporal the men in the stockade would sing a song to me when I went into the stockade to deliver the mail. It ran, "Look here my fellows, two stripes on his sleeve, he's a chicken shit corporal who does as he please". I thought this was rather touching.

## *A Civilian Again*

In mid summer of 1945, the Services developed a point system to discharge service personnel based upon their length of service, combat time, wounds and POW time. In November I reached the magic number and was discharged on Nov 19, 1945. With my duffel bag in hand and a "Ruptured Duck" (discharged symbol) on my uniform, I returned to Chicago, and to civilian life and again became Mr. Arthur F. Adams Jr. I then entered college on the G.I. bill, along with hordes of ex-service people, graduating six years later from the University of Illinois with a degree in engineering.

One of the first things my mother told me was to go and buy some clothes. How do you do this? "You mean clothes come in different colors?" The Army had given me everything up to now. I

113

then went to "Harry Levin's Clothing" store on Clark St. and he fixed me up. There were other changes such, as I didn't need a pass to go out at night, there was no reveille, I could put my hands into my pockets as long as I liked, and no calling people "sir" or saluting. There was, however, K.P. in the form of washing dishes at home, which I didn't mind at all.

Some one once asked me how this experience affected my life. Actually I am convinced that it helped make me a much better person. The medical problems resulting from long stretches of dysentery were resolved in about three years after a couple of trips to Hines Veteran's hospital. I required a considerable amount of dental work since malnutrition had an adverse effect upon my teeth. Most of my fillings had to be replaced and a couple of teeth had to be extracted. As far as my emotional situation was concerned being only eighteen when I went into service helped a lot. At that age feelings heal quickly. I did have some bad dreams but they went away after a while. Later when I attended the University of Illinois I looked into joining a fraternity. Even though I was only 22 I was completely turned off by their childish (at least to me) initiation practices and their emphasis upon partying. At this time all I wanted to do was to finish my education. For many years, however, low-flying airplanes made me nervous even to the point where I "hit the dirt" on a couple of occasions when planes flew closely by.

After dinner the first evening I was home I went for a walk with my dad and we talked about things that happened over the past

19 months. Except for the gray hair on my mother and high school classmates who were killed in the War, everything was the same. The cars were old, the neighbors the same, I enrolled in school again and picked up with my friends.

In a way it was as though I went into the army on a Tuesday and came home on Wednesday with my memories being nothing more than a long, hard dream.

# *Epilog*

In 1962 my company sent me to field assignments in Turkey and Pakistan. My routing took me through Europe. After reporting to U.S. Military representatives in I. G. Farben building in Frankfurt, Germany, I thought about visiting the site of the prison camps at Hammelburg. I didn't know if they still existed. Seventeen years before when I was a "guest" of the German government I was only 19 years old. At that age your memory often plays tricks on you and I wanted to see if the places I "visited" were really as I remembered them. I purchased a map of Germany and saw that the route to Hammelburg was straightforward and would take about an hour and a half to get there. I then rented a Volkswagen and set out on the autobahn towards Wurtzburg. The railroad yards, there, where I had worked, were all new and showed no trace of the war. The castle on the hill, where I was treated for shock after a British bombing raid was there overlooking the town as it had for several hundred years. There I turned off onto a side road leading to the town of Hammelburg. Being early November there was a light dusting of snow on the ground that made the countryside look as bleak as I remembered. Driving through Germunden I again stopped at a place where I worked as a railroad repair crewmember. Everything had changed. A freight train passed by on a track along side; the road pulled this time by an electric engine and not a steam locomotive.

116

There was no anti-aircraft (Flak) car following the engine this time! I couldn't help thinking that I hope that they had reworked the track we helped repair for their own safety. The repairs done by prisoners weren't always of the best workmanship.

When I reached the town of Hammelburg, which isn't very large, I drove into the town center. The town was bypassed by the war, which was fortunate since the architecture was of classical Medieval style. I drove to the railroad station where my memory became alive. Even though I had originally arrived there at night I remembered the station's facade. On the way into town I noticed a sign on a side road that read "Hammelburg Lager". Since "Lager" means camp in German, I turned off the main road and followed the side road up the hill towards the camp to see if this was the site of Stalag XIII. It seemed as though my memory had suddenly been restarted. I passed the building that housed the canteen where our guards had stopped for refreshment. About a mile further I came to a gate with a sign that read "Hammelburg Lager". The site was now a German army training post.

I parked the car and walked to the guard shack and in my best German I said to the young soldier on duty, that I was an "Amerikanisher Kreigsgefaner" and showed him my POW dog tag. After a few more sentences of butchered German, the infantry soldier politely asked me if it would be easier if I spoke English. With considerable relief I then told him that I was a prisoner here in 1945 and would like to visit the camp if possible.

117

The soldier then called a sergeant and explained who I was and what I wanted to do. The sergeant was about my age and had probably served in the German army during the war. When I showed him my POW identification tag he smiled and shook my hand. He gave his approval and detailed the young soldier to escort me about the area. Since it was now an army training post they asked me not to use my camera.

The soldier removed his pistol belt and opened the side gate leading into the compound. I told him he should leave his pistol belt on; it would make me feel as though "I was home." He laughed and said, "You don't have to put your hands on top of your head."

As we walked through the camp he told me some of the history of the area. The buildings were indeed built around the time of Bismark as a major training post for the German army. It was used during the First World War and well into the Second. The facility was now a major infantry-training center. When I told him that I, too, was a former infantryman he loosened up since there is a bond between infantrymen regardless of which country they serve.

He was not familiar with the camp's use as a prison camp. The guard towers and barbed wire fences were long gone. In a few places you could see the tower foundations. As we walked through the camp I pointed out the location of the French, Russian and Italian sectors, the British compound where they had a clandestine radio, the Yugoslav compounds and finally the two American camps. The old stables, which housed the enlisted prisoners, were still there but were now used as warehouses. When we approached the site of Oflag XIII I felt a chill, which was not from the cold weather. The buildings were refurbished but were still there in the layout and shape in which I remembered them. I pointed out the location of the barracks, now used to house soldiers, the camp kitchen and sick ward. When I pointed out the building in which I was housed the soldier took me on a tour through it. The inside was completely refurbished with single bunks and lockers. I pointed out the place where the old rifle racks stood which we prisoners took down and cut up for firewood!

After a walk through the parade ground where I shared memories about the "Schiesswagen," the morning "Apells", the "Goose Step" parade, the Serb and Croatian sectors and how they fought each other, and then to the building that housed the hospital where I worked as an orderly. When you looked closely at the brick area above the front door you could still see part of the words "Kranken Lazerette" or sick hospital. My escort said that he had not noticed that before. The building was now used for offices. I talked briefly of the "Baum" raid and the chaos that followed. In all of our discussions I never mentioned the lice ridden bunks, the poor food, the trigger-happy young guards, and the extremely cold living conditions. Nor did I mention the wagon carrying the bodies of the four POW's who tried to escape. He was a young boy when all this happened and as far as I was concerned these were all part of history and best left forgotten.

After our "tour" was over he took me to a soldiers canteen where he treated me to coffee. He motioned to a half a dozen other soldiers to join us. He then acted as interpreter. They were very interested in my stories especially about the "Baum" raid to liberate General Patton's son-in-law. They all had heard of Patton and thought he was a great General. We spent nearly an hour talking.

At dusk I said "auf weidersen" to the group and walked to the gate with my escort. The sergeant came out and chatted briefly with the soldier. They then shook my hand and we said our good byes. Then both men stood at attention and saluted me! This took me completely by surprise and I returned the salute. This simple exchange of feelings of mutual respect cancelled out all of the ill feelings that I might have harbored about prison life over the years.

While they watched me I walked to the rented Volkswagen, switched on the engine and drove away, hoping that the two soldiers standing there wouldn't see the tears in my eyes. During my trip back to the Autobahn the countryside now seemed to take on a sense of color which I did not perceive 17 years before.

# *Credits.*

1. Frontispiece. Author After Recovery. Author's archives.

2. Draft notice. Author's archives.

3. Daily Training Schedule. Fort Hood, Texas. Author's archives.

4. General Squier Class Troopship. Newspaper photo, 1945. Author's archives.

5. The Team. Combat photographer photo. Author's archives.

6. A town Like Kesternich. "Rhine, Roer, Ruhr" History of the 310th Infantry.

7. Battle of Kesternich. "Rhine, Roer, Ruhr." History of the 310th Infantry.

8. Cologne in 1945. Newspaper photo, Chicago Daily News, March 1944.

9. M.I.A. telegram. Author's archives.

10. Newspaper Casualty List. Chicago Daily News, April 1945.

11. P.O.W. notification. Author's archives.

12. Location of Major German P.O.W. camps. American Red Cross P.O.W. Bulletin.

13. Prisoners of War Bulletin May 1945. American Red Cross.

14. Hammelburg Liberation. Newspaper Photo.

15. Author as a Military Policeman. Author's archives.

Printed in the United States
17065LVS00004B/394-483